GIRLS IN THE CULT

GIRLS IN THE CULT

A Journey Into Self Discovery
by
FORMER OLD ORDER MENNONITE

Esther and Sarah in Galvanized Wash Tub
(1939)

Esther Royer Ayers

Library of Congress Control Number: 2013907516
ISBN: Softcover   978-1-4836-3029-8
               Ebook   978-1-4836-3030-4

Rev. date: 04/29/2013

To order additional copies of this book, contact:
Xlibris Corporation
1-888-795-4274
www.Xlibris.com
Orders@Xlibris.com
134951

Contents

1 Corinthians 13:11 King James Version

When I was a child, I spake as a child, I understood as a child, I thought as a child: but when I became a man, I put away childish things.

I dedicate this book to my
Wonderful brothers and sisters:
Mark, Grace, Ruth, Sarah, Frank, John, Paul

Some of whom, unfortunately, are no longer with us.

But we were all together at one time.
We walked through our childhood as one.
And, because we did this
We shall forever be one.

WE ARE THE PEOPLE OF THE PAST.

WE ARE GOD'S CHOSEN PEOPLE.

WE ARE THE ONLY ONES

WHO ARE GOING TO HEAVEN.

Until they become conscious
they will never rebel,
And until after they have rebelled
they cannot become conscious.

George Orwell in "1984"

....

Until they awaken
they will never know who they are.
And until they know who they are,
They will never awaken.

Esther Royer Ayers in "Girls in a Cult"

INTRODUCTION

Knowledge is beautiful. It unites rather than divides. Secrecy is controlling and weakening. Secrecy makes you walk on quicksand all the days of your life.

In my memoir, *Rolling Down Black Stockings*, published by Kent State University Press in 2005, I detailed numerous stories about growing up in a Christian church known as Old Order Mennonite. These stories honestly and accurately illustrated my oppressive childhood, and how the religion's numerous rules and regulations overwhelmed me at a very young age. All were designed to prevent me from ever leaving the religion.

At the time of publication, I still harbored mind blocks. I could tell you about the religion, but was ignorant as to why a religion would oppress its very own members.

I have not lived as an Old Order Mennonite since 1955, when I was seventeen. At that time, my mother undertook an unfathomable action for someone who had been born into, and lived as an Old Order Mennonite, for nearly fifty years. She, unintentionally, copied a story from the Bible, and, thereby, became a Moses of a Mom. With sincere conviction, she led her eight children out of captivity and into the Wilderness, the City in our circumstance. She was promptly excommunicated from her church.

The Wilderness that we entered into was actually the World, which hitherto had been forbidden to us. "The world is evil," we were taught. The world, in reality, represented the **present**—and we were required to live in the **past**.

When I entered the World, my mind was clouded with roadblocks as big as mountains—mountains I never knew existed. But isn't that characteristic of roadblocks? You can't possibly know you have them until you've broken through them.

In writing *Rolling Down Black Stockings,* I honestly depicted my story. Yet I wished, hoped, internally begged, that perhaps someday, someway, someone, somehow would come forward and say: *Esther, don't you understand? Your book is about such and such.*

Ah! I would exhale; my mind finally unclouded. *So, that's what it was all about.*

As you might imagine, no one came forward and said those words to me. Instead, when I met my readers at libraries, book clubs, festivals, fairs and events, they offered kind comments and honest critiques. And then they said, "Keep searching. You have another book within you."

My readers could not have said anything better to me, as those comments made me think deeper. Why would the people of a religion systematically program their children to fear the outside world? And worst of all, why would the people in a religion limit a child's education?

I first began questioning my childhood religion when in my young twenties, at a time when I was raising my two boys in the world. How differently I had been raised; how odd! And even when I tried to remember myself as a little girl, I could barely see her. She seemed so far away. And strange! Strange as she wrung her hands together! Strange as she lowered her eyes, barely risking a peek! Strange enough for me to ask: *Was she really me?*

Photographic memories of the girl playing with her siblings, of tending to chickens, of working in the garden, of crying from punishments, returned to me, but I didn't know her. *Was she really me?*

Meanwhile, commands pounded relentlessly within me, their words sharp and frightening: *Don't tell anyone on the outside about our religion. They won't understand us. They will harm us. And whatever you do, never write about our religion.* These commands made me ashamed of my childhood religion. What possibly could have been so wrong that I had to keep such secrets? All was bizarre, polarizing, and unsettling—and guaranteeing that I'd never speak or write about the religion.

But then, a few years ago, I met people who were like me. Oddly, they were the women who populated the ranch at El Dorado, Texas, the ranch called "Waiting for Heaven". I met these women through the medium of television. This incident prompted me to probe into the possibility that I may have been raised in a cult-like culture.

And, again, a year later I met someone like me. This acquaintance came through an invitation to participate in the first Tucson Festival of Books (TFOB), Arizona. The TFOB committee asked me to present my memoir,

Rolling Down Black Stockings, with a former Jehovah's Witness, Richard E. Kelly, author of *Growing Up in Mama's Club*. The committee cited many commonalities in our memoirs, and, indeed, once Richard and I read each other's book, we agreed. Most shocking was that Dick, as he prefers to be called, had grown up as a Jehovah's Witness in Los Angeles, CA. And I had grown up as an Old Order Mennonite in Columbiana, Ohio. Yet, basically, we wrote the same memoir.

A third part of my enlightenment came from my mother's diaries. I knew she had been writing diaries, but I had never read them until after she died. These diaries spanned the years from 1958 to 1989—from the year we moved to Akron until the year she died. Her stories baffled me, and prompted me to frequently ask: *How could she? Why did she?* Yet, I knew I behaved the same in so many, many ways. What did we have in common?

Old Order Mennonite women, and women of our sister religions, the fundamental Amish and Hutterite, are highly subjugated. When questioned about their dress, their hard work, their confining ways of life, they respond with "canned" comments such as: "Oh, we like living this way. God wants us to live this way. We don't mind it at all."

Such women have devastatingly low self-esteems and believe their words will be viewed as stupid. Their inner being tells them: *No one wants to hear what you have to say!* And worse—and far more damaging to their psyche—is that their oppressors have occupied a space within their heads.

Such women carefully watch their every word. They stutter, look here and there, twist the material in their dress, check, check, check their every word—afraid to say anything—then finally saying something—then fearfully adding, "Oh, I shouldn't have said that. I shouldn't have said that."

With eyes darting back and forth, already they've panicked, for they know if the tiniest tidbit of conversation finds its way back into their oppressor's ears, they'll have to pay. In their oppressor's ears, they know that tidbits, which meant little when uttered, will be woven into something big. Confessions will follow, and then punishments. Such women can never voice their thoughts or put their words onto paper.

In the year of 1953, my father died. He had suffered many years from the crippling disease of multiple sclerosis, and had spent his last seven years of life bedfast. Yet, after all this hardship, he requested the following momentous funeral song:

God moves in a mysterious way,
His wonders to perform.
He plants his footsteps on the sea,
and rides upon the storm.
Ye fearful hearts,
fresh courage take.
The clouds you so much dread.
Are big with mercy
and shall break,
with blessings on your head.

These words, written by William Cowper centuries ago, gave my father the strength and courage to endure his illness. My father passed these words of strength and wonder on to me.

I married my husband, Jim, in 1959. Throughout the years, he has provided me with a comfortable and safe nest. Within this nest, we were entrusted with two wonderful sons, Jim and Don. It was our duty to raise our sons with as many social, intellectual, and material assets as we could provide for them, thereby enabling them to go forward and have a good life. Let them build upon what we have given them, and let them pass all along to their children, and onto all future generations. Is this not the basic parental instinct of all living beings? Why would God ever choose to oppress his children through a religion?

An argument could be made at this point: God would not choose to oppress his children through a religion. This is true. God does not oppress his children. Mankind does. And mankind does it through the confines of a cult.

Another argument could be made: God gave us free choice. That's just the point: Being in a cult means you're under totalitarian control. You NO LONGER have free choice. What's God got to do with it?

NOTE

There are numerous and variously-named Mennonite churches that exist within our United States of America and throughout the world. Some of these churches are progressive and some are fundamental. Many of the modern Mennonite churches of today are involved in beneficial charity work.

In the pages of this book, I write about the Old Order Mennonites, the people of my childhood religion, the most fundamental of all the Mennonite churches. At times I may write OOM—or just plain Mennonite—but I am always referring to my childhood religion when I do so. If I should write about a different faction, such as the New Mennonites, I will identify them as such.

I was born in 1938 in a small farming community on the outskirts of Columbiana, Ohio. Our nearest big cities were Youngstown and Akron. These cities and the town of Columbiana are located in northeastern Ohio.

Born the fifth of eight children in a period of ten years, I am smack in the middle. Our community was cloistered because our religion was cloistered.

The photograph on the front cover was taken by Alta Royer (1907-May 5, 1940), my father's first cousin. She grew up on the original Royer (Reyher) homestead, which stood adjacent to the farm where my father was born and matured. This made them cousin-neighbors. Alta was never a Mennonite—and my father was not Mennonite until his teens.

Alta found my father's children irresistible photographic material. For this, I will forever be grateful. Alta captured life through the lens of her camera; I try to capture life through words on paper. Below is a photo of Alta E. Royer:

Alta took her own life in May 1940, at Massilon State Hospital, Ohio, a hospital that treated the insane. Since my three younger brothers were born after her death, they do not have photographs taken of them when youngsters.

I am asked, from time to time: "If your father could read your books, what do you think he would say?" I believe my father would say, "Esther, come sit by my side and read your books to me. Read your books to me one more time, will you?"

And then I'm asked what I think my mother would say. I believe my mother would throw back her head and laugh. Upon gaining composure, she would say, "Esther May, I just never know what you're going to do next. I just never know."

Neither my father nor my mother would ever have said, "We're proud of you!" Praise was never a part of my life.

AUTHOR'S DISCLAIMER

In this book, dialogue, in some instances, is used to create actual mood of an occasion. In other instances, it is used to communicate actual endeavors in simplest form. Always, dialogue reflects the voice of the people.

Additionally, at times in the following book's chapters, I will refer to my mother as simply "mother". If I am referring to any other mother, I will state clearly, "her" mother or "their" mother, etc.

PROLOGUE

As a young girl, when I complained about having to live such a harsh way of life because of my religion, my mother responded by saying, "Esther May, we are just pilgrims passing through this world on our way to our heavenly home. We do not look to our left, and we do not look to our right. We look straight ahead as we carefully follow the pilgrim pathway. If you think of it in this way, it'll be much easier for you to obey."

"But Mother," I said, "Not looking left! Not looking right! I might as well walk through this world wearing blinders. That seems like such a lonely way to live."

"But that's who we are, Esther May. We are pilgrims who must walk through this world all alone. We walk on a very narrow road. That's who we are."

I couldn't press further as a child, but could only accept. Today, however, I could say, "But Mother, doesn't that make us programmed people, programmed into perfectly-controlled robots, robots who respond but never think? Is that *who* we are?"

"Oh, no!" my mother would have answered, her eyes imploring mine. "Why, Esther May, why would you say such a thing? We are pilgrims who walk a narrow road as we travel through this world, a very narrow road, indeed. It's the only road that leads to God. We are not robots, Esther May. We have minds and we can think for ourselves!"

I should have said the following, but didn't: "It seems as if you're asking me to walk a narrow road where all I can do is zero in on little things in life. Like the many duties that litter my beaten pathway, concentrating on each step, daring not look left or right, keeping my eyes focused straight ahead—focusing on duties—focusing on the next step—and the step after that. If I do this, Mother, I'll never learn a thing. I'll never see the big picture in life.

"Life is about learning, Mother. It's about expanding your brain instead of zeroing in on little things. I want to know who you are, Mother, and I want to know who I am. That's what I want to know!"

PASSIVITY

Passivity makes you like Rip Van Winkle. While sleeping for twenty years, he missed some very important events in his life. He missed the Revolutionary War for one thing; and he missed his wife's death for another.

Whether you spend your days upon this earth asleep or awake, time doesn't care. Time will march on—with or without you.

CHAPTER 1

The Passive Pilgrim

When my Moses of a Mom led her children into the Wilderness (City), my youngest brother, Paul, was twelve. A short thirteen years later, when twenty-five, Paul wrote the following letter:

Postmarked Oct. 4, 1968, from New York, NY:

Dear Mom,

In your letter to me, which arrived this past Monday (Sept 30), you said that you had heard that I felt hopeless. You assumed I meant this in a moral or religious sense. I simply meant that I never expect to marry and raise a family, stick to any vocation in life, or, in other words, to mingle freely and feel totally accepted in society. I do not ever feel degraded, immoral, or sinful whether I am in a stockade or walking through a "red-light district." Guilt bothers me only if I sense that you-all at home have been hurt by my actions. My hopelessness is caused only by too few, too short-termed, and/or too shallow friendships now and through-out my past and future. I blame no one, only circumstances for this.

Paul was the youngest of eight children born into our Old Order Mennonite family. I am the fifth child—five years younger than my oldest brother, Mark,—and five years older than Paul. You could think of me as 555.

As children, we were terribly mind-blocked, isolated, and taught to keep the doctrines of our religion a secret. We were taught that the outside world was evil and would harm us. To keep us a separate people, we lived passively—as in the past—as in the same century of our ancestors, who had been martyred for their beliefs.

Only recently have I come to terms with who I am, yet Paul, as reflected in his letter, seemed to know himself at twenty-five. He knew he was a loner, but doesn't know why, and assigned his hopelessness to fate.

Perhaps Paul knew himself better than I because he had majored in psychology in college. Psychology has helped millions of people in the past, and is helping many people today. But can psychology help those who grew up in secrecy—secrecy harsh enough to cause mind blocks—mind blocks severe enough to get assigned to unknown circumstances—mind blocks rigorous enough to create robots—robots, those mechanical people groomed to be servants all their lives—those who are controlled by others and, thereby, can never be masters?

Some may argue that, when we become an adult, we can reflect upon our childhood and make good choices. I argue that one cannot make good choices when one has been prevented from growing the necessary brain connections to do so when a child.

I grew up in a religion so secretive that, if you asked my mother, my uncle, my aunt, the man up the road raking hay into stacks, or the lady in the garden picking strawberries for pie, "Who are you?" Each would stammer a programmed answer, "We are pilgrims."

"And, who is a pilgrim?" you might press on.

"A pilgrim is, well, I don't really know. We're just pilgrims. That's all."

While growing up in the religion, and for many years thereafter, I had thought we were extremely religious. I had thought we followed every word in the Bible to a T. In today's world we would be called extreme fundamentalists. As a child, I never heard such words. I doubt that today's Old Order Mennonites would use such self-descriptive words, either.

Instead of calling my childhood religiously-centered, I would call it rule-and-regulation-centered. We had numerous oppressive rules that we had to obey—most of them "do nots"—and all were punishable if not followed. These rules and regulations fashioned us into perfectly programmed robots—robots programmed to work rather than to think.

And work, work, work, we did. Because of our many jobs and chores, we didn't have time to read the Bible during the week. On Sunday, our day of rest, we should have had ample opportunity to catch up in Bible study. However, our church didn't believe in Sunday School or Bible study classes.

Church doors opened on Sunday mornings only. We listened to a sermon preached by a pastor who had no more than an eighth-grade education. He certainly wasn't going to add much to our knowledge on the Bible or religion. Audience participation was not allowed during this service; not even an "amen" could be uttered, our voices curtailed.

After church everyone attended a huge Sunday dinner in a member's home. Here, voices were freed—and rang forth with church matters and Bible matters and members' matters. Voices praised those still in line with church teachings, and reproached those who seemed to be falling by the wayside. The children used this time for play.

To mother's credit, she attempted to instill religion within her young children by reading *The Pilgrim's Progress*[1] to us after Sunday supper. This book is considered adult literature; therefore, as a child, I never understood much of it. But mother loved it, and read page after page with such fervor, her voice trembled at times. Her passion passed through to her children. The story is about a fellow named Christian who undertook a most breathtaking pilgrimage to find God. My mother suggested everyone should take such a pilgrimage in their life.

Other than that brief and shallow awakening, I walked with my mind blocked throughout my childhood years, my teens, my twenties, my thirties. Then, when in my forties, I attended college. Eventually, I obtained a degree in biology, with a minor in psychology. My studies awakened me somewhat—to the point that I knew something needed addressed, expressed and voiced. But what was it? Fear blocked any awareness that surfaced, that tried to sneak through, and so I slept on.

Nothing—nothing seemed to awaken me until a news flash blasted across my television screen in April of 2008. The images, raw and cutting, burned onto my brain, where they still glow today.

Oddly-dressed ladies wringed their hands in woe while parading up and down in a small paved area. They identified themselves as members of the Fundamental Latter Day Saints (FLDS). Their stories of anguish were wrenchingly sad, but I heard little of it. For immediately, and unfortunately, upon first viewing these ladies, I focused on their dresses.

Each lady wore my childhood dress, for heaven's sake—or a dress like I had worn as a child. *How dare these women wear my dress!* I thought—but for the briefest of moment—before more dreadful reports drew me into their anguish.

"Some four-hundred-thirty children have been rounded up, put on buses, and taken into custody by the State of Texas," the newscaster reported. "These children have been living on a ranch at El Dorado, called 'Waiting for Heaven.'"

Their reports planted images of girls nearing puberty, girls still young enough to innocently skip rope to favorite nursery rhymes. With each jump, the girls' hairs bounced freely in the air, with the sort of music and beat that make poets pick up their pens. Sadly, these girls weren't being watched by poets, who bring joy into this world, but by elders who were looking for a young girl to wed, to add to their already long list of wives.

And why would he need so many wives? Because his particular brand of religion said that he could have them, making him think that he *should* have them, and all because God needed people of *his* sort on earth to populate God's heaven.

The girls' mothers, their faces scrunched in pain, now told their sad stories on television. "The State took our children away," they wailed, rocking nervously to and fro. "The State claims abuse. There is no abuse here. Our men are good people. Our daughters are simply choosing to marry young."

They may have said more; I'm sure they said more, but I didn't hear it because, by this time, I was stuck *in* their dresses. It was my dress, after all, my childhood dress, and only good Christian pilgrims called Old Order Mennonites, people who sacrificed their lives here on earth, were entitled to wear this dress. We were the unique people; we were the ones having many children for God. And *we* did it all without having to share husbands! Monogamy made us the good ones, the ones going to heaven. How dare the polygamous FLDS claim our religious rights!

This news stunned me so much that I was unable to prepare dinner and clean house for days, maybe weeks, maybe more, I lost count. But when I saw those FLDS women wearing the dress of the Old Order Mennonite women, it slammed into my conscious brain with such ferocity that it cracked my cranium. Having a cracked cranium might seem bad, but, in fact, it was good. It was good because it gave me this insight: *Esther May, if FLDS women and girls wear your dress, and you know that FLDS is a cult, then maybe you grew up in a cult culture as well.*

Other thoughts coalesced and raced through my brain: Jehovah's Witnesses is a cult: my childhood religion said they were evil. FLDS is a cult: my childhood religion said they were of the devil. Our religion was the good one, our religion was true. We were God's chosen people; therefore, we couldn't be a cult.

Yet I saw what I saw, and the images of the FLDS women still walked through my brain. I simply could not deny that, if such ladies wore my childhood dress, they could be like me in more ways than one.

Television media quickly dubbed the FLDS garb as prairie dresses. Others called them pioneer dresses. Whether prairie, pioneer, or simply peasant dresses, these dresses were designed for the heavy work required in kitchens and in fields. Sleeves were gathered at the shoulders to ease movement of arms when picking fruits and vegetables in the orchards and fields. Sleeves were banded at the elbows for ease in digging, planting, hoeing, and weeding. A peasant, prairie, or pioneer woman or girl working in the field ended her day with a quick, cold wash-off at a hand pump, usually located outside her kitchen door.

When field work ended, a peasant's kitchen work began, and her dress served equally well there. Work began with a hatchet, the chopping off of chicken heads. It then moved to a bucket of hot water, where the chicken was dunked, making feathers easily plucked. Next, cutting around the rectum with a sharpest of knife, and then reaching inward, feeling, grasping, and a gentle twist of chicken's innards separated the entire gut package, which now slipped easily into one's hand. The art of cleaning chickens was learned by little girls when their wrists were the slimmest.

Prairie dress skirts had a dropped waist, which was fully gathered, long and loose, for easy bending in the fields. Closing in on the ankles, the skirts rendered legs and panties unavailable for glimpses, should a lusty man or two lurk nearby.

Prairie skirts also hid the dreadful plain bloomers of peasant women and girls, bloomers made without a hint of lace, lace, which could have quietly, delightfully, graced delicate bottoms without anyone knowing—had peasants been permitted such luxury. Instead, peasants contended with bottoms that had never seen the sun—or should never see the sun, as we were frequently warned.

Bloomers, stained with menstrual blood when a period began in the field, were endured, for no one dared leave, lest someone question why.

These long and loose skirts served another purpose as well, for hidden within their folds were babies, babies who ripened like the fruits on the trees and the vegetables in the garden, until ready to be picked.

I admit I haven't the faintest idea of what the FLDS ladies wear as undergarments, for they keep all well-hidden and unavailable for a briefest of glimpse. But I know what we wore, and surmise it was similar.

Our religion's peasant dresses were made of the most durable fabric, generally calico cotton, and imprinted with the tiniest of flowers on soft pastel colors, all of which eased laundry chores. Feathery lightweight fabric had another benefit as well, for it tended not to tire out the wearer. This was of utmost importance for women who labored from sunup to sundown.

The dictionary defines a peasant as someone who lives off the land, is hard-working, and has a harsh life. This certainly describes the life of a girl or woman in our religion. And, probably describes the life of the FLDS lady as well.

My mother's classification of pilgrims, as the people who walked alone, was certainly accurate. Indeed, Mother! You may as well have given me a rear-view mirror and said, "Esther May, if you look in there, you'll see who we are. We are those people who were born into the present world, but turned our backs on that as we walked into the past. Look! See us! See us walking away, becoming smaller and smaller. Someday, you'll barely see us at all. Obey God, Esther May, and obey your elders. Life will be easier if you'll accept."

Say "pilgrim" to most children and a picture of the Mayflower coalesces in their brain, a picture of our adventurous forefathers who bravely sailed the Atlantic blue under extremely harsh conditions. They sailed to reach a new land, America, to attain religious freedom.

A dictionary gives another definition of pilgrim, however, the definition mother meant. Her pilgrim was someone who undertook a religious journey, or pilgrimage, in search for perfection. Perfection is an illusion, a goal one can never obtain. It's the search for the pot of gold at the end of the rainbow. It's the journey that keeps one pious all the days of one's life.

Surprisingly, I learned we share many commonalities with the FLDS women. We both wear the dress of the past; we both live the hard life of working off the land. Other commonalities are:

(1) Most of our religious doctrines and practices are kept secret from the world.
(2) We bear many children.
(3) Our children go directly from diapers to helping out in the kitchen, to working in the fields, to milking the cows in the barn, and to serving as primary caregivers for younger siblings as they come along.
(4) Education is de-emphasized.

(5) The women's dress is plain and simple, and nothing we can purchase at Macy's. Therefore, we have to make them.

(6) Both are totalitarian societies.

(7) Women are subservient to men.

(8) (9) (10) Women are subservient to men.

Suspicions that I may have grown up in a cult drove me to google the internet. There, I learned about the most admired expert in the field, the famed Dr. Margaret Thaler Singer, who authored *Cults in Our Midst²*. How shocked I was to read that a favorite custom of cults was to separate followers from the world!

Isolation—the separation of OOM members from mainstream civilization—comprised most, if not all, of my childhood religion's rules and regulations. In modern-day America, innovation geared to making life easier flourishes at breath-taking speed. Yet Old Order Mennonites choose to forgo electricity, running water, computers, huge field tractors, telephones, televisions, and a myriad of amenities, all affordable and available, to embrace the hard ways of the past. Hours of leisure are considered to be wasteful, sinful. One must "work, work, work, 'til the day is done" as imparted in a favorite hymn heard in their kitchens and fields.

Dr. Singer also suggested a favorite custom of cults was putting forth strategies and doctrines to purposefully weaken its members. Living in the past certainly qualified as "weakening". Limiting one's education for religious reasons qualified as weakening, harmful, and anti-human. Wearing "different" clothing—where the women made all the "outies" and "undies"—qualified as a weakening culprit. And the required use of harsh and unpleasant outhouses qualified as a weakening culprit, as well.

Some readers might mistakenly question my use of "required" in the previous sentence. They may have believed we used the outhouse because we lived in the country. Or, they may have believed that we were too poor to afford indoor toilets. Neither would be true. We used the outhouse because church rules stated that we **must** use the outhouse, those relics of the past. Indoor potty-places were on the list of the forbidden, a list that contained indoor plumbing, running water, telephones, and a host of other conveniences, all used plentifully and frequently in the present world.

A favorite maternal aunt of mine loved to tell the following story regarding her parents and outhouses. "When my parents moved from Virginia to Ohio, they bought a home with an indoor toilet," she said.

"I don't know if they thought the Ohio church would be more lenient, or what went through their heads, but whatever it was, it was incorrect.

"As usual, the bishop moseyed around the home before the family moved in. When he spied the beautiful indoor toilet, he hurried to find my parents, who were renting nearby. He then shook his finger in my surprised parents' faces, and scolded: "Not allowed! Not allowed! Tear it out and build yourselves an outdoor toilet before you set foot in your house!"

My aunt continued her story: "My trembling parents tore out the sink and toilet, but didn't tear out the bathtub. We used the big tub as our mending box for all the years we lived there."

My childhood was without running water or indoor toilets. I never experienced such luxuries until we moved to Akron. By then, I was seventeen-years-old.

Experts state that a charismatic leader, whether man or woman, is always at the helm of a cult. At face value, this eliminates Old Order Mennonites, for their leaders, all men, appear most meek and humble.

If you visited one of their communities, you would have great difficulty identifying the bishop, the preacher, or the deacon (their hierarchy of leaders), for not one wears clothing any different from another man in the community. Likewise, all leaders and men in the community have occupations of farmers and carpenters.

One should not be lulled into sleepy delusion that all people within our community have equal power. Indeed, great power rests with the bishop, who, in the morning, can order all women to lengthen their skirts. By evening, all women will have lengthened their skirts, and the skirts of their daughters. Should this happen during the busy peach-canning season, peaches will rot until skirts are lengthened.

Neither should one be lulled into sleepy delusion that Old Order Mennonites have no charismatic leader at helm. To find them, you'll have to travel back in time, back to sixteenth-century Switzerland and Germany, to a time when the Catholic church ruled the land and peasants populated the fields, to the time when Martin Luther nailed his ninety-five theses onto the All Saints' Chapel door in Wittenberg.

In this time period, the Old Order Mennonite religion was born, although not named as such then. Their forefathers were called Anabaptist Reformists. These Reformers were charismatic, radical, and rejected Catholic doctrine and practices. They further believed that Luther's Protestant Reformation didn't go far enough. In particular, these early Anabaptists believed that infant baptism was wrong, and stated emphatically that baptism should be made by conscious choice, which can happen only when you're an adult. Additionally, Anabaptists wanted a separation of church and state, and a closer alignment with the teachings of the New Testament.

Some of their beliefs went against Catholic and Protestant teachings. Especially egregious were their pacifist beliefs, which led to their refusal to serve in wars. Within a few years, Anabaptists were severely tortured and martyred for their convictions. All has been documented in story and with accompanying etchings in *Martyr's Mirror*.[3]

Today, three religions trace their heritage to the Anabaptist Reformation: the Mennonites, Amish, and Hutterites. Doctrines originating with these early Anabaptists are in practice today, doctrines such as the believer's (adult) baptism, separation from the world, pacifism, a literal translation and close adherence to the teachings of Jesus and the Holy Bible, and the washing of one another's feet to show humility and respect among believers.

The martyrdom endured by early Anabaptist leaders still pulsates within pilgrims today. If "pulsates" could talk, they would say: *Martyrdom is the call that unites us all. We must never forget! We must never forget!*

Years can pass in our religion with no strong, charismatic leader at the helm. Yet, "pulsates" do not dim and clarion calls do not dull; indeed, these are the very motors that power faithful pilgrims' footsteps.

Centuries can pass with all motors finely tuned, and with clarion calls ringing sharply in air. Then, seemingly, out of nowhere comes an out-of-step pilgrim, who sees our religion as a neglected garden. "Too many weeds are clogging our pilgrim pathways!" he loudly proclaims. "I don't like this garden. I don't like it at all!"

His disgruntled disposition is as catchy as the flu. Another pilgrim steps forward and says, "I don't like this garden anymore, either."

Others join in, and their voices become many. "Plow this garden under," they proclaim. "What good is a garden with weeds?"

Dissatisfaction, at times, means a forward and modernistic movement—dissatisfaction, at other times, means a retreat into the past. Unfortunately, with my childhood religion, dissatisfaction meant a hurried retreat into the past.

Jacob Wisler was a dissatisfied and disgruntled preacher. He proclaimed Sunday sermons should be delivered in German. He proclaimed Sunday School should be abolished. He proclaimed children should be taught about the Bible at home. He proclaimed evangelism had no place in religion. He proclaimed the church return to the ultra-conservative times when men controlled women—head and shoulders, knees and toes.

Those already basking in the kind breezes of moderation, and those already strengthened by the enriching winds of knowledge, protested such talk. "Take your ideas and go home! Jacob Wisler," they said, in words loud and adamant.

But others invited Jacob to stay.

This caused a schism in the church. As usual, one schism gave birth to another, and when all the schisms were counted, there were many, indeed. Some called themselves Martin Mennonites, some Wenger, some Weaver. To the outside world, all looked like Old Order Mennonites, but those on the inside knew the subtle differences.

Subtle differences, such as how women wore their head-covering strings! Flimsy strings that men made into mountains. Oh, how should our ladies handle them? the men fretted. Should they be tied under the chin or allowed to hang loose? If loose, should strings lie on bodice fronts or be tossed to the back? While men debated strings, the women, who had been made clever through hardship, and made shrewd through silence, retired to the kitchen to bake a cake.

There, the women peeled apples and beat eggs and laughed and sang and chatted about their children. Soon the cake was put into the oven to bake.

Meanwhile, the men discussed their dilemma in the adjacent room. Soon one appeared at the kitchen door, sniffed the air, and then exclaimed. "My, is that an apple cake you're making!"

Another joined him. "Emma, is that your recipe?"

Still another asked, "Is that your good apple cake?"

"Smells like it's ready," said Emma, as she took the cake from the oven. "Anybody want a warm slice?" Her rosy cheeks, glistening from the heat in the kitchen, accentuated the white bow of her covering string, which, incidentally, was tied neatly under her chin.

Suddenly, all became clear. "Our women will wear their covering strings tied neatly under their chin," said one man. The others readily agreed.

The above story is illustrative, and never took place, as far as I know. Since I am a woman, I would never be in on decisions regarding the arrangements of covering strings, and whether one should tie them under the chin, or not. But I do know that the Old Order Mennonite men make such decisions, and I do know that the Old Order Mennonite women are terribly clever and work wonders to have things go their way.

In fairness, censorship of dress was not limited to the women in our community. Since men were not allowed to wear belts, they wore suspenders. And since zippered flies were forbidden, men wore buttons to keep their flies shut. These buttons, by the way, were considered adornment for women, and forbidden to be worn by them. But, since men's were hidden—well—who can figure the how and why of some of their rules? But, once a rule was passed by the leaders, everyone in the community had to comply.

ELITISM

Elitism is the two-sided fence of isolation.
Elitism fences you in.
Elitism fences others out.

CHAPTER 2

The Elitist Pilgrim

Fences can be found in the oddest of places. A fence can even be found in an Amish buggy, such as the one being driven upon a curvy, country road in upstate New York, such as the one encountered by my Florida Optometrist, Dr. Smith.

While living in Florida in the early 2000's, I visited Dr. Smith's office for my customary checkup. Experience had taught me to arrive early, and to bring along an interesting book, for the wait could be an hour, even longer, at times. Armed with my latest reading material, I was deep into its pages when called into his office.

On the book's front cover was a colorful, garish photograph of an Amish couple stacking bales of hay onto a flatbed wagon. The gaudy cover seemed out-of-place, for I knew the Amish people as non-showy, as people who sought to remain in the background of life. But the brash cover did as intended, and caught Dr. Smith's eyes as soon as he entered the room.

"I'm familiar with the Amish," Dr. Smith said, as he upped my chair to facilitate my eye examination. He then chuckled as he positioned my head so that it nestled comfortably within his cushiony rest. While fumbling through his examination tools, he chuckled more, then found what he needed, and proceeded to blind me with his bright light. *What's so funny?* I wanted to ask, but before I could get a word out of my mouth, he began telling his story.

"My family and I took a vacation in upstate New York earlier this month," he said, and chuckled.

"It's woodsy up there, full of trees, full of vines, and full of narrow, curvy roads. These roads can be dangerous if one isn't careful. You have to take them slow." He chuckled some more.

"While driving on one of these curvy back roads, we came upon an Amish family in a horse and buggy. I couldn't pass them because of the narrow road, so we followed the buggy for some distance."

Needing to change tools, Dr. Smith stepped to the side and fumbled through his optometrist toolbox, chuckling while fumbling. Obviously, whatever had happened amused him greatly.

Upon finding the correct tool, Dr. Smith continued with his story: "As we neared the back of the buggy, we had a clear view of an Amish boy. He had positioned himself in the buggy's back window. He probably was three or four, somewhere in there, just a cute, little kid.

"Anyway, as we approached nearer, the boy up and stuck his tongue out at us. He stuck his tongue out at us," he repeated, now openly laughing. "You know how kids are, *ha, ha, ha*. I have kids of my own, so I know how kids are."

At this point in the examination, Dr. Smith had my head tilted back and was shining his light deep into my eyes. I made *Umm! Umm!* sounds, the sounds one makes when needing to say something, but can't. It's like being at the dentist's office with a wad of cotton in your mouth, then being asked a question. I was forced to take an alternative move—to take a "road less traveled" sort of response—and rolled my eyes. I agree it's a dumb thing to do during an eye examination, for such a move could get you hauled off to the hospital before having time to offer a sensible defense.

Dr. Smith seemed oblivious to my signaling attempt, and continued with his story. "The boy's mother didn't think that her son was funny, however. She up and yanked him from the back window and pulled him into the buggy. Then she yanked that heavy, black curtain shut, you know, the one they have in the back of their buggies. It's thick and it's heavy. She yanked that shut!"

My doctor laughed heartily about the Amish boy sticking out his tongue, then dismissed it all with: "You know how little kids are. Children will be children."

I wanted to comment: *You have this all wrong! This is not a matter of children being children.* But, Dr. Smith seemed so happy with his vacation discovery that I hated to burst his floating balloon. Indeed, if this incident had been a simple case of children being children, the mother would have reprimanded her son with the following: "Sticking out your tongue is wrong. Now, wave your hand at the nice people in the car." Is this not what any normal family of the world would have done?

In my opinion, my eye doctor had innocently witnessed an Amish toddler's lesson in isolation. The toddler learned his world was made up of good people and bad people. People who had buggies were good, and people who had cars were bad. His mother reinforced her son's lesson when she pulled him back into the buggy and closed the curtain.

As youngsters, most of my siblings and I were quite timid. Conversing with strangers made our eyelids weighty. Looking into a stranger's face would have been an impossible task. Sticking out our tongue would have been a feat that was light-years away from our ability to accomplish, or even think about.

Nonetheless, because we were bashful and incapable of sticking out our tongues doesn't mean we were incapable of separating our worlds. Indeed, it does not. Our mother, a true stickler for our place in this world, snapped our heavy black curtain shut when she uttered these words: "Children, there are good people in this world and there are bad people in this world. We are the good people. Always remember that!"

She continued her diatribe with: "Children, take pity on the bad people of this world. After all, they can't help it that they're going to hell. They simply were not born into the true and righteous religion."

Believing that you and your religion have been chosen by God to be favored above all others is religious elitism. All seems haughty and snobbish, and smacks of high self-esteem, characteristics not found in humble and lowly Mennonites. You would think with such knowledge, we, as children, could have opened our eyes wide. We could have looked at strangers without shyness. However, we couldn't do this because we didn't feel elite. In fact, we didn't feel special at all.

If one examines elitism with a fine-toothed comb, one will be surprised. Elitism actually benefits isolationistic religions, for it keeps members from ever leaving. If you left your religion, God's favorite, where would you go? To go elsewhere would be frightening and dim-witted. And we weren't dim-witted at all.

When living in the OOM religion, isolation blocked my mind from knowing much about the outside world. The reverse was, undoubtedly, true as well. How much did the outside world know about Mennonites?

My knowledge about this subject was scanty when my memoir was published in 2005. Subsequently, through talking to book club groups, libraries, and at book festivals, I have acquired a better understanding. In one of my book club talks, an audience member told me an especially revealing joke. The joke follows:

> *A Baptist died and went to heaven. As St. Peter showed this Baptist around, he noticed a group of people standing alone, and off to the side. The Baptist asked St. Peter who those people were, and the Saint said they were Mennonites. He quickly added, "Don't tell them you're up here. They think they're the only ones."*

Imagine how shocked I was to hear this little anecdote. The world does know about Mennonite elitism after all!

In jest, let me assure all Baptists and other religions of this world that there is no need to worry about available space in heaven. Not since the great news has come out, that is. Did you know that our universe is expanding? Expanding means enlarging, which means heaven is enlarging as well. Heaven no longer need be limited to Mennonites. Soon there will be room for Baptists, of which there are many. And soon there will be room for all.

I began this chapter questioning a colorful book cover that displayed an Amish couple stacking hay onto a wagon. The cover seemed deceitful to me, for Amish do not permit photographs to be taken of them. The prohibition of photographs is true with the Old Order Mennonites, as well as a few other fundamental religious sects. These religious groups believe photographs represent the "graven images" that are specifically forbidden by God in the Second of His Ten Commandments.

I noticed on the book's cover that the Amish couple did not look directly into the camera. *Smart!* I thought. If need be, this couple could feign innocence, should they be hauled up in front of their congregation for disobeying rules. When asked to explain the picture, they could have exclaimed: "I didn't know the picture was taken!" They could then confess their sin of innocence and all would be forgiven. If they refused to confess, the bishop could charge them with disobedience—a serious charge—one that could result in shunning by family and church members. Shunning is more painful than a spanking for plain people; and, undoubtedly, more painful than death.

In the Old Order Mennonite religion, the prohibition of photographs is under the "thumb" of a bishop. Most powerful, a bishop determines whether photos are evil or good within his particular community.

On the cover of *A Heritage that Money Can't Buy* is a beautiful wedding photograph. This beautiful couple is my maternal grandfather and grandmother, the parents of my mother and of my Aunt Sarah, the author of the book. You can view this cover by going to my website: *www. EstherRoyerAyers.com*

In her book Aunt Sarah explained that photographs were once permitted by the church. When the old bishop died, a new bishop came into power. The new bishop declared that photographs were evil and all must be burned. Church members made haste and complied with his order, some reluctantly dragging their heels, as can be expected, but, finally, all were tossed into the fire. Well, not quite all. One had escaped, and was hidden away by a female cousin.

The cousin wisely surmised that the severe bishop couldn't live forever. Perhaps, a new bishop would be more tolerant. Perhaps, he'd declare photographs were not evil. After all, a photograph burned is a photograph that can never be retrieved. She silently hid her copy away.

All came to pass as the cousin had surmised: a new bishop issued a new rule stating photographs were allowed. As the cousin grew old, she gave the hidden wedding photograph to my Aunt Sarah, and said, "It was just too beautiful for me to throw into the fire." Indeed! Indeed!

Photographs give one identity for they clearly say: *I was here upon this earth.* Pilgrims do not want photographs that prove they were here upon this earth. According to their belief, they're just passing through.

Passing through doesn't mean pilgrims are **not** interested in genealogy, not at all! They're not interested in just anyone's genealogy—but in their genealogy—the true genealogy—which might enable them to trace their roots back to their wonderful, wonderful past—back to the days when Anabaptist Reformers walked upon this earth—back to the pilgrim martyrs' days.

If you were to find yourself in a pilgrim home, you would find genealogy books which appear to sleep on shelves. But, if you looked closely, you would find these books are very awake and alive. You would find a book had been opened as recently as yesterday. Fresh ink would have recorded a new birth, a name and date, and there it would join a multitude of carefully preserved and maintained names, identities that stretched back into previous centuries.

Pilgrims have found great security and comfort in knowing that their names occupied these silent pages. Finding their name nestled, and comfortably linked with the many generations that had come before, verified they were on the proper pathway. Their religion was true and right yesterday. Their religion is true and right today.

Although my childhood religion didn't believe in the photograph, they did believe in recording pages of history in time.

Diaries, written memories, photographs, genealogy records, historical documentaries, and tree rings all speak of identity. All say: *I was here upon this earth at one time. And such and such happened while I was there.*

Since evolution is defined as the changing of life as it moves through time, photographs and tree rings are actually visual representations of evolution. And diaries, genealogy records, and histories are written representations of evolution.

As I tried to think through my mind blocks caused by my childhood religion, I turned to social psychologist. Dr. Eric Erikson, (1902-1994), and his "Eight Stages of Life". These stages are commonly referred to as ages: the "Eight Ages of Man". A google search will quickly bring up oodles of links to websites on this subject,—or you can go to the original source. In Dr. Erikson's book, *Childhood and Society* [4]—Chapter 7 in particular—you can read about these stages.

As we progress through life, according to Dr. Erikson, we acquire specific socialization-development skills at certain ages. A list of the eight stages and ages follows:

1. Trust or Mistrust—Birth to 18 Months
2. Confidence or Doubt—18 Months to 4 Years
3. Initiative or Guilt—Years 4 to 6
4. Industry or Inferiority—Years 6 to 12
5. Identity or Confusion—Years 12 to 18
6. Intimacy or Isolation—Years 18 to 25
7. Growth or Stagnation—Years 25 to 40
8. Integrity or Despair—Years 40 and Beyond

As a child I loved playing a game of school on the fourteen stairs that led from our parlor to our upstairs bedrooms. My siblings and I sat with rapt attention on the first stair—while an older sibling asked us a question. If we answered correctly, we were permitted to move up one step. If not, we had to stay behind. This mimics passing through grades in a school.

Dr. Erikson's eight stages of social development differed from our game of school, as played on our stairway. We moved ahead—up one stair—if we answered a question correctly—and only if we answered the question correctly. In Dr. Erikson's stages, you moved ahead regardless of whether you've answered correctly, or satisfied the criteria, in his case.

The difference between my childhood game of school and Dr. Erikson's stages is:

In my childhood game, only by getting a "right" answer were we allowed to advance. In Dr. Erikson's Stages, advancing to the next level was independent of whether you achieved the stage. Instead, advancing to the next level was entirely tied to time.

When a tree writes its rings, the tree doesn't have to pass a certain agenda in order to write its next ring. A tree writes rings in good years and in bad years. Tree rings are a record of how life was in a specific location and at a specific time.

Photographs also record how life was for a person, place or thing in a specific unit of time.

Since time always moves forward, and never backward, neither a tree nor a person will ever have an opportunity to rewrite an event.

In my life, I can never rewrite events and experiences. For instance, I can never rewrite the following:

(1) My baby, toddler, and adolescent years were experienced as an Old Order Mennonite.

(2) During my childhood years, I witnessed and experienced my father's battle with Multiple Sclerosis, the progression of his disease, and his untimely death, when I was fifteen.

(3) I have seven siblings; I am in fifth position; we were born within a ten-year span of time.

(4) The Old Order Mennonite one-room schoolhouse, that had served our community, closed the summer I was to enter first grade. This event necessitated that I attend public school, which placed me in a world outside of my isolated, religious community.

(5) My mother's disillusionment with the Old Order Mennonite religion, and our family's move to the Full Gospel religion, happened when I was seventeen.

All of these events, like tree rings, are written whether right or wrong or good or bad. As a tree can never rewrite its rings, neither can I rewrite any of my childhood Stages. Unlike the tree, because I am conscious and intelligent, however, I can look back and see how these past events made me into who I am today.

Time always moves forward, which makes all life unique. Every new baby that comes into this world is carrying a new gene combination that has never been upon this earth before. And, at the very moment that a new baby is born, a new wave laps upon an ocean shore—a wave that has never been upon this "changed" shore before—the shore having changed because of continuous shifting sands. Therefore, baby, wave, shoreline, and sand are all new for this particular moment in time.

We notice visual differences in generations and assign labels such as Generation X, Generation Y, etc.

Humans reflect upon their changes and ask, *what if?* What if this had happened instead of that? The "what if's" are numerous. The best we can do is assign them to answers that are "blowing in the wind", as Peter, Paul and Mary sang.

Dr. Erikson's Stages do not deal with "what if's"—but with what was.

What was? That's the stuff recorded in photographs and in tree rings.

I carry some childhood memories in my head, which return to me in photographic fashion. One such memory has me walking into the kitchen. I'm very distressed for I cannot find my mother. I'm so little that I can walk under the table, and see the giant table legs. I feel lost and frightened.

I cry, maybe I scream, that part isn't clear. But I clearly see and hear what happens next. Someone runs into the kitchen, grabs me from under the table, and carries me to a nearby room. It's not mother—and I don't know who that someone is. Nevertheless, I feel comforted.

Years later, I learned that Mother had taken my brother John with her when she went to Virginia and attended her mother's (my maternal grandmother) funeral. John, born in 1941, was three month's old at the time. Since I was born in 1938, this means I was three-years-old at the time. Yet, I can replay the photographic memory of myself under the table. I can even experience the same feelings—my sadness and fear when lost—and my contentment when found.

Years later, I learned that not only had I been left behind, but five of my other siblings had been left behind, as well. We were in the care of our father. Already ill with the beginnings of multiple sclerosis, my father found his job bigger than he could handle, so had called in neighbors to assist him.

A photographic memory of a different time in my childhood involves my oldest brother Mark. It is suppertime, and we are sitting around the table. Mark fusses and refuses to eat his supper. Mother gets up from the table and makes him some junket. (Junket, a store-bought, rennet product, is recommended for stomach and abdominal distress. It comes powdered in a box much like the pudding mix we purchase today. When stirred into heated milk, it turns into a custard-like food.) Mark likes the smooth and soft feel of junket on his tongue, and seals his contentment with satisfied noises.

Mother makes many "special" dishes for Mark because he refuses to eat otherwise. When he tries to eat chicken or anything made with eggs, he makes gagging sounds, turns up his nose, then looks at his siblings, and asks: "How can you eat such stuff?" He then makes guttural sounds, shakes his head, and shivers. His words and his actions splash across our supper table like slop, making his siblings ill and unable to eat, as well. It's easier for our mother to make junket for one child than to have a table full of children who can't eat their meal. But our father disagrees and tells her she shouldn't do this. My mother does it anyway.

Grace, my second oldest sibling, twists her curly blond hair around her fingers whenever someone comes around. She fidgets with her skirt, making sure she keeps it down. Mom calls Grace a good girl because she does this. She's also called a good girl because she loves to cook and relieves Mother of much kitchen work. At the tender age of five, Grace makes meals for her family while Mother tends to her latest baby. Grace, already, shows the markings of being a good wife and mother.

Ruth, my next sibling in line, hates to cook and wants to work on the farm. "You're a girl," mother says. But Ruth begs persistently until mother relents. When Ruth is not at the barn, but home, she chins herself on a branch of elm in our backyard. "I'm trying to get muscles," she says as she chins. "I want to be as strong as my brothers." She pauses long enough to catch her breath, then says, "Come on, Esther. Try it. You can do it. See!" She flexes her muscles. "See! You can get big muscles like me."

I try, but can't make one lousy chin-up. I realize that I'm a "fanny" girl—a girl who prefers to sit on her fanny and read. It doesn't upset me one little bit.

My sister Sarah is next: she's thirteen months my senior. Sarah was born breech, which caused a back injury. She crawled on the floor until two. My parents then took her to a chiropractor in town, who made some sort of adjustment in her hip and back area. She stood up and walked. Since, by that time, I walked as well, mother referred to us as twins.

Sarah and her breech birth were responsible for the telephone we had in our home. It's atypical for Old Order Mennonites to have a telephone, which they feel is too modern and will bring evil into their homes. During Sarah's long birth, my father had to go to a neighbor to telephone the doctor. In the meantime, Sarah arrived. Father blamed himself for Sarah's birth difficulties and had a telephone installed.

My three younger brothers, Frank, John and Paul, can rightfully claim that I taught them every childhood game they know. And they can thank God for an older sister who liked to play more than work. My intelligent mother quickly saw value in this: I became her major live-in-babysitter.

Since Frank and I began our first "hired-out" job together, I feel bonded to him in a special way. As youngsters of eight and six, we walked up the graveled Germantown Road that ran by our house. Our legs became heavier as we approached our workplace, (actually, an OOM home/farm) where we would work for the next few weeks, months, and, in Frank's case, years. Neither of us would have guessed such a possibility on that day. Frightened as we walked into the unknown, we felt like Jonah entering the mouth of the whale. In passive resignation, we did the only thing that we could. We kicked up dirt as we neared our workplace—stalling our entry as long as possible.

Although I taught and played games with John, I had more responsible tasks with him, such as making sure he stayed on his potty chair. He viewed this task as a time to play, and transformed cereal flakes into trains. Zoom, zoom went his train around the tray. "Zoom, zoom!" he said. "Zoom, zoom!"

"Has he done anything yet?" Mother yelled from the kitchen.

"Not yet," I answered.

"Then keep watching him, and don't take your eyes off him for one single second!" she ordered.

"Hurry," I coached John, but he didn't hear me. He was lost in creation, and made his train stronger and longer. His tray filled with concentric circles of cornflake cars, aligned in dizzying arrays. When he began eating his train-car, I knew he was done.

The first time I saw Paul, our youngest sibling, he was wrapped in a blanket. His blue eyes opened wide as he was introduced to his seven brothers and sisters. He was then whisked away by mother and placed in a cradle in our parents' bedroom. Each time he appeared, he was wrapped in his soft blanket. My sisters and I crowded him, begging to hold him, but mother was afraid we'd drop him. So, we tickled him under his chin, hoping to tempt a smile. He rewarded us, but we didn't stop. More tickling and more crowding until our mother whisked Paul away into the safety of his crib in my parent's bedroom, and closed the door.

One day when Mother brought Paul into the kitchen, two chairs had been set up next to my parents' bedroom door. My father appeared in the doorway, and with labored walk, took one chair. Mother, with three-month old Paul bundled in his usual blanket, took the other.

Father tried to convince Mother to put baby Paul in his arms, but Mother was reluctant, fearing that our multiple sclerosis-stricken father might drop Paul. But Father begged and coaxed until Mother did so. Once Paul was anchored securely within his arms, he looked down at baby Paul, and laughed with delight. And Paul looked up at his father and smiled. Just like that! He smiled without being tickled under his chin by his sisters until his skin reddened.

Mother soon became fearful and took Paul out of Father's arms, retreating once again to their bedroom. It seemed as if I didn't see Paul again until we played school on the stairs. He was a very good student and passed up the stairs quickly, advancing much faster than anyone could have done in Dr. Erickson's stages. He was a good student, indeed.

Photographic memories, although precious to me, are static, maybe biological tissue, and will pass away when I'm gone. But photographs and written words, now digitalized, makes their end impossible to guess.

ATTIRE

Dressing alike takes away your sense of self.
It also takes away the sense
that one person is better than another.

CHAPTER 3

The Disciplined Pilgrim

When giving talks to groups of people at libraries and book clubs regarding Old Order Mennonites, some have said to me: "Leave these people alone. They're hurting no one. They make mouth-watering soft cheeses beyond compare."

Some in Tucson, where I now live, have said, "Have you ever tasted queso menonita?"

Others have said: "No one can make a better pie than these ladies."

Still others have said: "They're peaceful, honest, and hard-working. When I see them laboring in their fields, or see them in marketplaces selling their garden and farm products, their baked breads and pies, they seem happy enough. Actually, they seem like little children, so leave them alone."

I agree with the cheeses, the pies, the hardworking assessments. And, I most wholeheartedly agree that they seem like little children. Virtually, they are little children, for they have very little control over their lives.

Old Order Mennonites believe that one should *not* spare the rod, for failure to do so will spoil the child. Totalitarian control techniques can act like a too tightly-laced corset, and stunt emotional and social growth. Excessive discipline used to make children obedient often results in fearful children, children who retain childlike ways to please adults, children reluctant to venture into novel play or to think of new ways to handle chores, preferring to stick within the "safe" tried and true.

Dr. Erikson's study of early childhood years presents a window through which we can see how children get locked into childhood ages. Although their bodies mature physically into puberty, teen, and adult stages, psychologically and socially they remain in a child state.

In my particular case, when I was in Dr. Erikson's Stage 1—Trust or Mistrust—Birth to 18 Months—I would have met my four older siblings on the day I was born. Crowding around my cradle was my oldest sibling, Mark, a five-year-old lad. Peeking around Mark, and jostling for viewing position, were my sisters: three-year-old Grace, two-year-old Ruth, and thirteen-month-old Sarah. It must have been quite a welcoming committee that greeted me into this world—four siblings, five and under—peeking at their newest sister.

When in Dr. Erikson's Stage 2—Confidence or Doubt—18 Months to 4 Years—three boys had been added to our family: Frank, John, and Paul. This made a grand total of eight. Eight children born within a ten-year period in time would have been a houseful for my parents under normal circumstances. But we didn't have normal circumstances in our household. We had an ill father who had a progressive disease.

When my first sibling, Mark, was born, my father walked with a limp; when my youngest sibling, Paul, was born, my father used a cane. As his disease progressed, claiming legs, arms, speech, and eyesight, he gave up his livelihood of carpentry and farming. More claims upon his body forced him to give up driving his beloved Ford. Then, when I was eight, news came that his father (my paternal grandfather) had been killed while crossing the busy Highway 14 that ran by his farm. Upon being told the dreadful news, my father collapsed onto the floor and had to be carried to bed. He was bedfast from then on, too incapacitated to even attend Grandfather's funeral a few days later.

*   *   *

Rolling Down Black Stockings was published in 2005, at a time when I lived in the Tampa Bay area in Florida. Soon, thereafter, the library in New Port Richey, invited me to speak about my newly-released memoir. The audience was composed of friends, those interested in literature, those interested in memoirs, those interested in religions, and those who collected books by new authors.

The group was highly attentive and found my story about growing up Old Order Mennonite interesting and surprising. After my presentation, I asked for questions and comments. A lady in the audience raised her hand, and said, "It must have been very cozy growing up in your community."

I replied, "To be honest with you, it wasn't cozy at all. I would describe it as confining, for it was a place where everyone had to watch his or her actions and deeds, but I would not say it was cozy."

"But, but I mean, I mean with all those brothers and sisters, you'd never have been alone. I grew up as an only child, and, believe me, it can be very lonely growing up that way."

I realize the outside world thinks that growing up in an OOM community and home is cozy, for that is the image presented. Many siblings, a year apart in age, means someone is always available for play. But remember, the "Little Old Woman Who Lived in the Shoe" and with all her many children, "she didn't know what to do". Does anyone believe it was cozy in there?

I am most grateful for my seven wonderful siblings, and fondly remember our happy play-days. However, we were groomed to be pilgrims, pilgrims who walked alone, pilgrims who did not live cozily together. We cried alone, we prayed alone, and we suffered pain alone. Feelings of sadness were never shared with one another, and neither were feelings of happiness.

At no time did I come home from school and share my hurt feelings when teased about my dress. At no time did I come home from school and share happy feelings when my teacher praised my spelling paper.

Anger was never voiced in our home, either. Loud words were never said. A fist banged on the table, accompanied with a voice that rang sharply, yelling: "I'm so mad, I could . . . I just could!"—was never heard.

Angry outbursts would have been cured with a couple swipes of rubber hose across our rump. And, we'd be sent to our bedroom where we'd stay until the next morning.

Tears were treated as shameful. If we had to cry, we cried in our bedroom, alone, our tears dampening our pillows, wet pillows sharing our grief, wet pillows sharing our pain, wet pillows offering us comfort and softness without accusation or complaint.

Voicing doubt or questioning any facet of our religion, or anything said in the Bible was positively not allowed. Should a sister err by questioning, I was taught to report her. Thereby, I became an unwilling monitor enlisted into the punishment of my own sister.

Karen Armstrong's outstanding memoir, *Through the Narrow Gate,*[5] details her entrance into a Roman Catholic convent in 1962. As a novice, preparing to be a nun, Karen endured seven years of harsh training and discipline. Being a nun gives the image of living in coziness, but her story is one of confinement and aloneness. She left the convent ill and disillusioned.

While reading Karen's memoir, I realized the discipline training she endured was similar to the discipline training my siblings and I went through to become pilgrims. I list these similarities below:

(1) Karen, the novice, was not allowed to question her Catholic religion in any way. If she committed this transgression, all the other nuns-in-training were required to tell their Superior. Karen learned to keep all thoughts to herself.

1-a: As mentioned a few paragraphs earlier, my siblings and I were not allowed to question our religion. And, we were required to report on a sibling who might have asked a most innocent question.

(2) Karen was not allowed to express anger, love, touch, or share secrets with her religious peers. Hurts were not shared between one another, but endured alone. Feelings were not discussed with any other person.

2-a: Such severe stoicism was true for us as well.

(3) Humility was prized above all else.

3-a: This was true for us, as well.

(4) Karen was taught that first, and above all, you were here upon this earth to serve God. Secondly, you were here to serve others. You were *not* upon this earth to serve yourself, or to even think about yourself.

4-a: We were taught these exact same words.

(5) Karen, when studying to be a nun, was taught to monitor other students and report misbehavior. If a Superior suspected suspicious behavior, Karen was brought before this Superior and questioned in depth.

5-a: Reporting misbehavior was true with us as well. We had to be honest, for a lie would result in an even harsher punishment. Ratting on a sibling was difficult, to say the least, but we could take comfort in knowing we were doing the right thing. Such comfort was quickly crushed when we had to watch the punishment inflicted upon the one we had reported.

Watching a sibling punished because you reported him or her was mentally painful—more painful than taking the licks of a whip yourself. All seemed a prelude as to what would happen once we joined the church and Confession was carried out before church members.

Karen mentioned in her book that the pain of having to watch those she reported endure punishment caused a deadening of her feelings. I can relate, and I totally agree with Karen's conclusion.

(6) Karen was allowed a weekly bath, and such a bath amounted to more of a reddening-of-the-skin-scrubbing than a gentle relaxing bath. Soaps used were harsh and the water likely cold.

6-a: We also took a bath once-a-week, which seemed more of a scrub-down. The water was generally cold and the homemade soap was harsh. Baths were taken on a Saturday evening, and in the privacy of our cellar. A galvanized tub was filled once with warm water (an example of our tub is shown on this book's cover). Those entitled to take the first bath or two were fortunate to have clean and warm water.

Baths were taken alone, for, it would have been most egregious if one of us saw another naked, whether of the same sex or different. Females went first, and the males followed. My brothers would have remembered bathing in cold, dirty water, while my sisters and I experienced a slightly warmer bath.

(7) Karen was permitted one dress (uniform) in the laundry per week—as was each novice. On Sunday, Karen and the others changed into a fresh dress.

7-a: We were permitted one dress per week in the laundry as well, and we changed into a fresh dress on Sunday. These rules also applied to the males, a shirt and overalls, in our family.

(8) When becoming a nun, you were required to promise that you would never leave the Order.

8-a: The above was true for Old Order Mennonites as well. When joining the church, new initiates promised they'd never leave the religion.

(9) Karen mentioned that silent prayers were said at meals. Karen further described that nuns were not allowed to eat with people of the world, for eating with someone implied a sharing of values.

9-a: We, also, said silent prayers at all meals. And we were taught to be careful with whom we shared meals, for who you ate with indicated a sharing of values.

(10) Karen was taught that manual work occupied one's hands—which allowed the mind to be free for God thoughts. Therefore, manual work was good.

10-a: We were taught these exact words.

(11) Karen was taught that reading fiction was a waste of time, and not allowed. Reading material was selected and approved by Karen's Superiors.

11-a: We were not allowed to read fiction either. As a child, I never read a Mark Twain or Jane Eyre book, or many of the other books that enriched the lives of other girls my age.

(12) Karen, as a novice, and I, as a pilgrim-in-training, shared many rules of silence and punctuality.

12-a: As Karen noted, we were to be quiet at the table; we dared not be late; we ate everything on our plate without complaint.

Promptly, after the meal was eaten, we cleared the table of dishes, washed and dried them, then put them in the cupboards.

(13) Karen was "hooded" when she took her vows and became the Bride of Jesus.

13-a: Old Order Mennonite girls began wearing their "head covering" when they joined the OOM church.

(14) Karen learned to exist in very little space, and had few personal items.

14-a: We were allocated very little space and allowed few personal items. As girls, we each had one small drawer in our bedroom dresser, in which we kept personal items.

The similarities Karen and I shared while she was a nun-in-training—and I, an OOM girl-in-training—were (are) stunning. Perhaps, most stunning of all is the fact that I was taught that Catholics were wrong—and, if you were a Catholic, you would not go to heaven, but would surely go to hell. I strongly suspect Karen was taught that all religions, except Catholic, were wrong, and all non-Catholic members were sinners and would not go to heaven, either.

People who live in controlled confinement have great needs for escape. Some means of our escapes were commendable and worthy, such as the quilting parties that took place in our homes. We strove to make the tiniest, matching stitches, thereby feeling a great deal of satisfaction, maybe even a little superiority, in our finished product.

Crafting—the carving of wooden toys, which could be considered fun work—provided men with a splendid escape. Sometimes the men built little pieces of furniture, a chest with pull-out drawers, a dresser with a tiny mirror on the top, tiny high-chairs, and rocking chairs.

Quilting and crafting produced useful products—a value most essential for pilgrims, who, with their silent "Waste Not, Want Not" banners never heralded, never paraded, but existing within their cloaks of frugality, all the same. Pilgrims, quietly treading upon their lonely pathway, exemplifying beauty in quality, crafted art that makes others gasp.

A phrase mother often recited to her children was, "Time should not be wasted!" Wasting of time was seen as counterproductive to the pilgrim life. It would be like asking a bee to take time out for tea. Life on earth is short, mother communicated in word and deed. Whether you're here to make hay or honey, it's all the same.

Pilgrims and bees have another commonality as well. The buzzing that bees do while working in their hives is analogous to the singing that womenfolk do while working in their kitchen.

The women in my childhood community preferred gathering together to tackle a big task. Preparing food for a barn raising would be one such example. As they peeled potatoes, prepared chickens, snapped beans and made pies for thirty or so men at times, the women sang as they worked. In this setting, you could rightfully call them efficient little factories, or you could call them a hive of busy bees.

When daughters were old enough, about four, they joined their mothers in song. Even young girls sang hymns while shelling garden peas, snapping green beans, or grinding corn. It was joyous in the kitchen with everyone singing together while working together.

By far, the major escape for OOM men and women took place on Sunday after morning worship service. At that time, everyone gathered at *one* home for Sunday Dinner and visitation. Excitement about this escape filled every woman's thoughts, for no woman knew for certain who would be chosen until after church. This excitement would be comparable to a woman of the world vying for a "Queen for the Day" title in a most humble way.

To be asked to host the Sunday dinner might make a lot of work, but work never entered an OOM woman's mind. She sang as she spent Saturday afternoon baking pies, pickling hard-boiled eggs, and fixing other foods not needing last-minute preparation. Being chosen as "hostess for the day" without being prepared was unthinkable.

A young daughter, who might rather play than spend Saturday afternoon cooking and baking, could rightfully ask: "Why do we have to do this every Saturday, Mama? It makes no sense. We do all this work and you still never get picked. I'd rather spend time embroidering my sampler."

Her mother would patiently explain, "It's because we might be chosen. Do we want to be chosen and unprepared? How would that look? Let's work without complaining, can we?"

The selection as to who would be honored went like this: After Sunday worship service, women milled around in groups, then flitted from one group to another. One could almost see wishful words of *Please pick me; please, let it be me,* hovering in hopeful balloons above and around their heads. Such competitive words might seem unbecoming for a humble and passive woman. But, these floating words were never expressed; but felt. Words never expressed could not get one into trouble.

Although no woman in the community was above the man, a subtle hierarchy existed amongst the women. Suddenly, a woman from this group yelled: "Dinner at Joe Miller's."

All conversation stopped as folks turned their attention to this announcement, and then quickly departed for that home.

All was not so happy at the chosen member's home, however, not in the chicken yard, that is. While the happy wife rejoiced, a few plump chickens lost their heads, danced their last dance, and enjoyed a hot water bath without ever knowing. After a good plucking, thorough cleaning, and hurried stuffing, they were jammed into ovens. The aromas created while these chickens roasted put everyone into a most talkative mood.

"You heard about John Martin's pigs, didn't you?"

"No, tell me what happened."

"They got jaundiced. Yellow as could be. All of them got rejected."

"You don't say!"

"Yep! That's what I'm saying. All of them rejected. They told him to not even feed them to his family."

"Then, how about to his pigs? Could he feed them to his pigs?"

"Huh! You mean pig eating pig? Of course not! Had to shoot 'em all. Fifty pigs it was."

"Dinner's ready!" someone yelled from the kitchen. While everyone enjoyed a most scrumptious meal, much gossiping took place. Gossip served as a favorite form of escape for OOMs. Although condemning in nature, it provided the "holier than thou" release, so necessary for those who live in black-and-white worlds.

After the delicious and generous meal, men-folk gathered in parlors on winter days—and on porches in the summertime. They selected their favorite rocking chairs and picked their teeth while they talked about farming.

The women gathered in the kitchen and washed dishes while sharing women's concerns. "Who's going to help Thelma with her seventh baby now? She's due any day. Hope it's not twins. But seeing the size of her, could be, don't you think? Could be triplets, even, considering her size.

Goodness, how could she allow herself to get so heavy? She'll pay for it someday."

All this was said without rolling of eyes, for OOM women were too honest to do that.

Another woman spoke up, "You heard about Mable, did 'ja? She was heavy, too. Had her third stroke now. Knows nothing, does nothing, just lies there with a blank stare. So sad; it's so sad. And only sixty-two. Thank heavens she's got sixteen children, four who never married. They'll be a big help to her now. It pays to have lots of children, some not married." All this was substantiated with an honest round of sighs.

It was a good day for the woman who had been chosen as hostess-for-the-day. Somehow, through it all, she maintained her humble exterior. Yet, a win is a win, regardless of culture or religion. Those who listened carefully were rewarded with laughter that rang sweeter, and feet that stepped higher, a noticeable difference that, despite all the grooming and training, one could not erase.

All women are human, after all, and bound to the human-species instructions carried within their DNA: *To survive is to be smarter; to survive is to outwit.* It matters not whether one is giving birth to the most beautiful baby on earth, or on whether one has won the "host-for-the-day" award, a woman is bound to get heady from time to time.

A woman who wasn't chosen could view her loss as having to eat whipped cream on spinach for a few days. The "whipped cream" part was all the food she had prepared, which meant leftovers until midweek. If shrewd enough, by adding thickeners such as tapioca, she could extend the leftovers for an extra day or two.

All this would give her ample time to finish embroidering that pillow case she'd been making for daughter Martha's hope chest. Martha was seventeen now, and Charles had been smiling at her during church service. She saw him do so that very morning. Who knew how soon Martha would need pillow cases of her own?

As for the "spinach" part, a woman not chosen could divulge in dreams for a better day: Which meant she had to cook her little heart out on Saturdays from now on; which meant she had to cook all day.

All people, at their barest, are members of the human race, regardless of their religious façades.

When troubled as a child, mother told me to go into my bedroom closet and pray. "God will help you with your problems," she said. "God will be your strength." I went into my dark closet and tried to pray, but never found God there.

Rather than solitude with God, the dark closet emphasized my aloneness. I didn't think of God as someone who loved me, but as someone to be feared. After all, God doled out extremely harsh punishments at times. If bad, He could even send me to everlasting hell. I didn't need more fear for I had enough of that in my life. I needed someone who would wrap her warm arms around me and give me a big hug when I felt troubled. I needed love.

I didn't think of mother as a person of love, for she had never embraced me when times became rough. And she had never hugged me when I was sick. Instead, I viewed mother as someone too busy to listen to my hardships, but **not** too busy to dole out harsh punishments when I disobeyed.

I wished mother would have allowed me to sit on her lap while she tenderly brushed my hair. Instead, she insisted upon parting my hair rather severely in the middle, then making two strands into rigid braids. Could she not once have praised its softness? Could she not once have complimented its tawny color? Could she not have sensationalized its softness, its shininess, and trilled endlessly upon its thickness? Instead, she made braiding my hair a harsh, rushed-through experience. I would not have any softness in life.

My mother believed in saying her prayers in a dark closet. She had joined the OOM church when in her late teens.

My father, however, chose to say his prayers on his knees at the edge of his bed. I know all this only because I had asked mother about the necessity of a dark closet. She explained, "On our honeymoon, your father wanted us to say our prayers together. I tried kneeling at the edge of the bed with him. I honestly tried. But I just couldn't do it. So I went into the closet and prayed. Your father felt hurt about this, but I just couldn't do it his way. I just couldn't."

My mother was the pilgrim in our family, my father the non-pilgrim. Although equally paired in intelligence, their backgrounds were as different as water and rock. My father grew up in a home where religion was not important. His mother (my paternal grandmother) was a Lutheran—and his father was agnostic, bordering on atheism.

My mother and father would have been strangers in most circumstances; however, they lived within the same farming community.

Living close to one another did not mean they attended the same school. My mother, the pilgrim, attended the one-room OOM Germantown Road schoolhouse, just up the street from where I was born. My father, on the other hand, attended Cherry Fork School, a public school.

Living within the same farming community did not mean the two families engaged in the same livelihood, either. Indeed, their livelihoods were as different as rock and water, also. My maternal (OOM) grandparents owned a chicken hatchery; while my paternal grandparents made their money through dairy farming and by raising crops, such as potatoes, wheat, and strawberries.

It was in the strawberries fields that my future parents, Fannie Rhodes and Walter Royer, made eyes at each other. Or, as my mother modestly explained, "He liked the way I picked strawberries."

In Ohio, strawberries ripened to picking quality in the last few weeks of June and the first weeks of July. Then, picking season closed for a year.

First, a few strawberries ripened on the vine, which were quickly picked and consumed by the family. Within a few days, the entire field ripened. The bright red berries against healthy green leaves looked as colorful as red lights on a Christmas tree. Pickers needed to be hired, for strawberries, an impatient fruit, were at optimal quality for a few days only.

Farmers hustled to hire as many hands as they could while strawberries were at their prime. Fortunately, my grandparents knew where the peasant-pilgrim girls lived. And they knew these girls would work from sun-up 'til sun-down without complaint. In fact, these girls, better known as Old Order Mennonite girls, would work like grasshoppers in their strawberry fields. They worked in pairs, one working the near side of a row, the other working the far side. Hunkering low, these girls began their row. All you could see were their heads. Well, not actually their heads, but their pastel-colored calico sunbonnets. These sunbonnets had brims big enough to be umbrellas, which nicely kept the sun off the girls' faces. The back ruffles on the bonnet were full and deep, which properly kept the sun off their necks. The long sleeves on their cotton-calico dresses protected their arms from the sun. Bonnet, dress and sleeves was all you could see going up one row, down the next, which gave all an appearance of grasshoppers gleaning a field, some very good grasshoppers, indeed.

As many as forty grasshoppers would appear for work at times. With two working per row, twenty rows were picked at one time. These grasshoppers worked diligently as they picked the berries, disappearing into rolling hills, reappearing in other rows. Disappearing, reappearing, disappearing, reappearing in shallow valleys, all providing a nice rhythm that moved like waves across the field. Wooden flats filled with quart baskets of strawberries appeared at row ends. Hundreds of quarts, to be honest, appeared in no time at all.

Along the edge of the field came the happy farmers, their horses pulling flat-bed wagons. The farmers loaded the filled flats onto their wagon, but first took a strawberry for taste. The strawberry's cocky green cap was quickly pinched off, and the red strawberry disappeared into the farmers' mouths. Soon, red juice dripped from mouth corners. A mushy "Y-m-m-m," is all you would hear, while the farmers reached for another and another.

With wagons full of the mouth-watering strawberries, the farmers headed to the towns of Columbiana and Leetonia. There, anxious towns-people waited, lining the streets. They cheered as the horses appeared. Already wives had shortcakes baking in their ovens and fresh cream chilling in their iceboxes.

Towns-people jostled for first place in the line, but no one went home disappointed. Everyone enjoyed strawberries for supper, and ate strawberries for breakfast, dinner and supper for the next few days, as well. Some even bought extra quarts, ten extra, twenty extra, which they put up in jams and preserves to be consumed during the upcoming cold, winter months.

One grasshopper, who had picked strawberries, would eventually become my mother, and the farmer who had hired her would eventually be my father.

Dutifully, mother listened to her six-year-old daughter's question: "Why do we have to go into the closet to pray if God is everywhere?"

She patiently responded, "It's because we are humble people. Words said out loud can lead to pride. We seek an individual and personal relationship with God in quietness and without boastful or showy words."

I thought, but did not say: *Isn't this the same reason you give me regarding silent grace, Mother, the silent grace we offer God before our meals?*

Her answers left me unfulfilled at times, and I wondered if she knew what the rules meant. Did she simply repeat words that her mother had told her? Perhaps, she, like me, merely obeyed.

Our religion's desire for humility revealed itself most openly at Sunday morning worship service. Members used separate doors to enter the sanctuary. Men, dressed in black collarless suits, their white shirts peeking an inch at the neck, entered from the left. The women dressed in plain somber colors, generally black, matching their black bonnets and stockings, entered from the right. Silently and solemnly members filed into rows of hard benches, benches separated by a generously wide middle aisle that kept the sexes separated. The men and boys occupied seats on the left-side benches, the women, girls, babies and toddlers of both sexes, took seats on the right.

Prayers were said quietly, with everyone dropping to their knees.

A sermon was humbly offered by the preacher, in laborious fashion, for he, a member from the same flock, had learned the same lessons regarding humility and pride, as had his parishioners. As such, no preacher possessed the gift of public speaking.

The churches environment changed superbly when hymns were sung. Everyone stood for these, cracking the kinks out of their backs when first standing, which served as a tuning fork.

With lungs fully expanded, silence was broken with volcano-like suddenness. Joyful voices filled the air in song, and the congregation quickly mimicked the mood. Members smiled to the people on their left, then to the people on their right. Unable to cap their singing joy to these few, they turned around and smiled to the people in the rows behind them. Singers in the rows ahead of them turned around and smiled at them. All this smiling and singing made everyone joyous and happy, as joyous and happy as a tree full of birds suddenly bursting forth in song.

Some hymns do not lend themselves to joyful communication. An example would be: "Asleep in Jesus, blessed sleep." These hymns were sung reverently, and with the respect they commanded. A solo, duet, or quartet was never performed at an OOM church service, for no member was viewed as better than another. "Singling out one, two, or a few people to perform a song would lead to pride," said our mother.

Musical instruments were not allowed in the church or in our homes, either. My mother offered this reason: "Esther May, God loves a cheerful voice, and musical instruments are not voices!"

Always interested in her children's religious welfare, our mother read her Bible to us on Sunday evening. She quickly tired of it, however, and switched to her favorite book, *The Pilgrim's Progress* by John Bunyan, which I've mentioned earlier. This book, an allegory written in seventeenth century England, is highly prized and still in print today. My mother's edition of the book was four-by-six-inches, the size of a prayer book. It was bound in burgundy leather, with a gold-imprinted shield and a gold-imprinted border. A handwritten notation on the first page stated the book had been given to her by her parents, my maternal grandparents, when she was a teenager. This would have been around the time she joined the OOM church, in the early 1920's.

My main education about God and Jesus did not come from *The Pilgrim's Progress*, however. Neither did my education come from the Bible. Nor did my education come from attending church, which we did infrequently due to our father's illness. My main education about God and Jesus came from the many hymns mother sang throughout the day.

These hymns seemed to serve as valium for mother, and I received some of the valium as well when I sang with her. In the beautiful neither-here-nor-there-land, we sang *Blest be the tie that binds, our hearts in Christian love; the fellowship of kindred minds, is like to that above.*

When we sang hymns together, I felt love. I felt love for mother. I felt love for our past relatives who now rested in churchyard cemeteries marked with plain, humble gravestones: simple squared or rounded-top stones that stood no taller than a rolling pin. I felt love for our pilgrim-martyrs who had come before us, and who had walked the same pathway upon which I now planted my feet, pilgrim-martyrs who had endured and kept the faith by keeping their eyes focused upon God, and not upon things of this world, pilgrim-martyrs who authored the beautiful hymns I now sang.

Singing meant sharing hymns with the very people who had written them. Singing showed me my assignment in life. If I walked the same pathway as did my ancestors, I could be strong. I could endure, as they had done.

Although the valium-uplift I received from singing hymns eased my day, I still hated my endless chores. My mother, on the other hand, loved mixing hymns and work together. One of her favorites, which she sang many times throughout the day, was *Work for the night is coming, work through the morning hour.* As if reminded by the song, she'd spot some work that needed done, such as a basketful of apples on the kitchen floor. "See those apples, Esther May?" she'd point at them. "Those apples have to be peeled today or they'll rot."

"All of them?" I'd ask, incredulously, my valium gone.

"Why sure!" she'd respond, adding robot-helper words, "Waste not! Want not! Always remember that, Esther May!"

I hated all the work, hated dusting furniture Saturday morning, hated baking pies Saturday afternoon, and hated washing the kitchen floor Saturday evening. I hated peeling potatoes every morning for breakfast. But the job I hated most of all was washing dishes, which was exactly the job I had to do most often.

At times I'd flatly refuse to wash the dirty dishes, which earned me a spanking. It also earned me a "bad" label, as discerned by mother. Once when I refused to wash dishes it turned out to be good. You have to be careful for life can trick you at times. If I had washed dishes on that particular day, I would never have learned that cows had no opportunity to worship God.

Instead of washing dishes, I went onto our front porch and sat on the swing. Creak, creak, went the swing as I swung back and forth. Should I be a good girl and wash those awful dishes, or should I stand my ground for once in my life? The problem seemed monstrous.

Across the gravel road the cows mooed in the evening meadows, and then nibbled on green grass: their snack before settling down for the night. Nor fair, I thought, they don't have to do dishes. Perhaps people should nibble their food off the ground, as well.

From the porch swing I could see our beautiful front yard, which was full of soft, green grass. The grass enticed me to come and recline upon it, to contemplate my dish dilemma. While flat upon my back, I could see God's vast blue sky, the place where I was taught that God lived, the place where I would join Him when I died, which made me wonder why I had to go into my dark closet to pray.

The cows mooing in the meadow diverted my attention. Some, already lying down, had tucked their legs under their bulk, their heads now bobbing left and right. How sad, I thought, that cows couldn't lie upon their backs, as I did, not until they died, that is. Did a cow ever get to see the beautiful blue sky? How would cows know that God lived up there if they couldn't see heaven?

Then I wondered why cows couldn't go to heaven, for I had been taught that only people could go there. And people only went to heaven if they were good. Which, right now I wasn't, since I had refused to wash the supper dishes.

It just didn't seem fair that I could be good and go to heaven, but a cow could be good and not go to heaven. Maybe a cow, never bad, never worried about an afterlife. Yet, I had heard comments that seemed to indicate otherwise at the breakfast table. "Bessie was stubborn again, couldn't get hardly any milk from her today. I gave her a good smack on the back."

Or, "Moon Face went through the wrong gate again. Stabbed her with my pitchfork. It bled, bled too much, but maybe she'll learn this time." It seemed I was always hearing about a bad cow. Bad cow whacked upon her back. Bad cow mad, put down, so sad.

The cows I watched from my place on the grass seemed content, their legs tucked beneath them. As they chewed their cud, their calves, played nearby, kicking up their feet and prancing around their mother just to show her they could. Then, as if they needed to touch base, they darted toward their mother, nuzzled into her belly, and then pranced away again. It seemed that cows and calves had such a loving connection; this nudging mother's underside, sniffing her soft underbelly, then testing the world once again. A nip, a couple of nudges, a few sniffs, and baby calf was off and running, happily prancing across the meadow once again.

All this nudging, sniffing, and snuggling made me long to give mother a hug . . . but my dreamy wish was shattered by a screeching screen door. There, appearing on the front porch was mother. Twilight had settled in, requiring that she cup her eyes with her hands as she scanned the horizon. She found me. "Esther May! Come in this instant! These dishes won't wash themselves, you know!"

I tightened my legs and drew my arms close to my body, trying to make myself into a stick. Mother, cranky from a full day of work, was not in the mood for games. She called louder, "Esther May! If you don't come in this instant, one of your sisters will have to wash the dishes and you'll be punished!"

Aha! A spanking was something I could endure. I decided to ignore her call.

She called again, this time with more urgency, and mentioned a new kind of punishment. "Come in this instant or you'll have to miss your supper tomorrow!"

Supper? Tomorrow? Did I care about tomorrow when my tummy was full today? I think not, my mood flippant with newfound cow discoveries.

Time passes quickly when a punishment awaits you; a day can pass in an hour. When the next evening came, I had hoped mother had forgotten her threat. I tested her memory and set a plate for myself on the supper table. She was not amused, and reminded me that, since I hadn't washed dishes on the previous night, I wouldn't be eating. Instead, I was to take my chair and sit in the corner in the adjacent room.

There, I sat alone while my family ate supper. I was close enough to smell the roasted chicken, the flaky biscuits, the cooked peas, which, incidentally, were the peas I had picked that very morning. My poor stomach cramped, but my heart outright ached. I felt like the bad girl confined to a confession chair. Was this a taste of what was to come?

While sitting there, pouting, feeling sorry for myself, I wondered how Mother could sing nice hymns with me on one day, and subject me to ugly punishment on the next. Was this how God worked: His wonders to perform? The truth was that, since I didn't have much opportunity to learn about God, He didn't seem real to me.

My mother, on the other hand, was real, and I loved her and feared her and assigned her behavior to the Old Woman in the Shoe. *There was an Old Woman who lived in a shoe, who had so many children she didn't know what to do. She fed them some broth and she fed them some bread, then spanked them all soundly and put them to bed.*

Surely her tiredness was caused by her religion, by her need to bear many children to populate the next generation of pilgrims. And surely, since only pilgrims could go to heaven, there was much need for people like my mother here upon this earth. All this would fall upon my shoulders someday, and I'd probably have to live in a "shoe" as well. As for now, it was best if I stayed out of her way.

Staying out of mother's way proved impossible, as I was soon to learn.

Upon walking into the kitchen on that fateful day, mother picked up the corner of her apron and wiped her tired eyes. She then allowed the cloth to linger over her nose, as if trying to find the girl she once was, the girl she had been before she entered the "shoe". She was a teenager once, after all; she was a new bride; she was a new mother of a son, then four daughters, then three sons, and all had to fit into her "shoe". Children crawling on the floor, children crawling out the door, children crawling up the stair, children crawling everywhere! Perhaps, with her apron over her nose, she could find a bit of solace. On the other hand, perhaps she needed to hide from her children. Surely, mother needed valium-hymn downtime, but had no time for hymns on that day.

She noticed my torn dress as soon as I walked into the kitchen, and lashed out: "Look at your dress, Esther May. Look at what you did! You play too hard! That's why you tear your clothing!"

Her harsh words affronted and frightened me. I wanted to defend myself and say: "*It's no big deal, Mother. This is my everyday dress. Who cares if I have a rip here, a tear there?*"

More angry words lobbed. "I'm going to make you a burlap dress," she declared loudly. "Let's see if you can wear that one out!" I'm sure she said more, much more, but by then I had stopped listening.

If I could have defended myself with words, I would have said, *Scratchy burlap is the color of dirt, Mother. We use scratchy burlap to cover our lettuce beds in early spring. And we use scratchy burlap to store potatoes, carrots, turnips, and other root vegetables in our basement in the fall. Burlap is harsh, Mother, heavy and scratchy. Burlap should not be made into little-girl dresses.*

I could have, should have said more: *If you'll remember correctly, my three older sisters all wore this dress before me. It was threadbare when I first put it on.* But I, a disciplined pilgrim girl, having been groomed to be stoic, having been groomed to be passive, having been groomed to be non-confrontational, had no voice available when truthful words were in order.

The burlap dress was scratchy and stiff, and made my previously light and merry "skip-to-my-loo's" become "skip to my logs". My valium hymns became barium hymns. Gone was my blithe spirit, my sweet laughter, all characteristics that had enhanced my younger brothers' lives. I turned into a glum, sulking girl, who ate until she was fat.

Fat hosted in other problems as well, for mother didn't like fat children. To her fat meant lazy—and lazy meant imperfect—and perfection, in the eyes of the church, was every pilgrim's goal. She called me fat and lazy to my face, which didn't bother me. In fact, I barely heard her words, barely knew she was around, my plumpness acting as my cocoon.

Inside my cocoon I was happy, for I no longer was a poor, pilgrim girl who wore a burlap dress. I became a fancy girl instead, one who skipped around the house in dresses with collars edged in lace, and with buttons in all shapes, sizes and colors. How beautifully they decorated my bodice and straightened my backbone! I even wore ruffles on my butt—and skirts so short you could see my satin panties, all make believe, of course. In my mind I ditched my black stockings, and wore white bobby socks.

Amazingly, cocoon life enabled me to think clearly, much clearer than I had ever thought before. For instance, I deduced that corn and tomatoes would protest, and even refuse to bear product when forced to bed with weeds. I deduced a mending basket would groan and break if not relieved of its heavy load in time. And I deduced that I might appear fat to mother, and that she might even call me lazy at times, but if she could have seen what went on inside my head, she would have deduced I wasn't lazy at all.

And, best of all, since I no longer fit into my skinny, older sisters' dresses, when school rolled around I gained two new cotton calico dresses of my own.

*   *   *

In the wee morning hours, while townspeople slept, country cows mooed. They needed to be fed and they needed to be milked. Children, usually males, were assigned to cow chores, while females handled kitchen duty. In our household, one sister, Ruth, joined her brothers in barn chores, an argument she had won years earlier with our mother. "I don't like cooking," she had complained rather loudly. "It's too simple for me." With four daughters in a row, and with a second and third son too young for heavy farm chores, mother relented. "Help out at the barn if you must!"

Always! It was always the wee, morning hours when our mother called up the stairs, "Children, get up!" Her voice, resounding in the early morning coolness, grew louder with each step. "It's time to get up, children! Get up!"

We should have answered: "It's too early, Mother! Have yourself a cup of tea! Go back to bed for an hour!" Or, we should have once protested, "Sorry, Mother, I'm not doing this today!" But protests such as these, forbidden, were never uttered in our home. Instead, we blindly crawled out of bed, stumbled into our work clothes, and began our day.

My brothers and my one rebellious sister, comprising the farm troop, were first up. They quickly dressed and moved out the door, not pausing for hot chocolate, which was not made—nor for a cup of tea, which was not made either. They could have sneaked a piece of bread but were too conscientious. So, without food or drink, they headed toward the barn.

Once they stepped out the door, they took whatever the good day offered. Sometimes they stepped onto ice-crusted snow; sometimes they stepped into buckets of pouring rain, and rarely, although most welcomed, they stepped into a perfect day.

On such perfect mornings, the troop walked with high, bouncy steps, and dared a couple of two-steps, maybe twenty-three or more, along our graveled road. They twirled and twirled until dizzy, then giggled as they struggled to stay upright. In the country darkness, with only a moon watching their behavior, they loosened their censored feet and tasted freedom, the freedom that children of the world enjoyed.

Dancing put the troop into a most jovial mood, so jovial that it continued when they tossed hay in the loft. There, they played one potato, two potato, three potato, four. Here comes a rake-full down to the floor.

Still in their jolly mood when they milked the cows, they played one potato, two potato, three potato, four, again. One pull, two pulls, three pulls, four. One pull, two pulls, three pulls, more. All made pleasant sounds as milk pinged into the buckets, then ponged into their buckets as they filled. Playing this game while milking made work downright pleasant, made work downright pleasant, indeed.

When it came to scooping up the debris that the farm animals had deposited in their straw beds overnight, my siblings couldn't come up with a game.

Meanwhile, my sisters Grace and Sarah helped Mother in the kitchen. Mother, the first riser in our home, already had coals burning in the stove before calling up the stairs. When my sisters joined her, they filled pots with water and placed them on burners, then scooped dabs of pig lard into cast-iron frying pans. On some mornings Grace and Sarah stirred ground cornmeal into boiling water for cooked mush. On other mornings they peeled, shredded and fried potatoes, rendering them crispy-brown on the outside while steamy, soft, and white inside. Frequently, we had fried sausage or ham with eggs. Since mother detested runny yolks, we scrambled or fried all the eggs until they rubberized.

The general rule in our home was that we ate what we grew in our gardens or on our farms. This meant that if you grew up in northeastern Ohio you didn't have orange juice for breakfast, or any other fruit juice. And it meant you didn't have an orange or any other citrus fruit either. We didn't bother with Vitamin C for breakfast, but were healthy just the same.

My job was to gather the eggs in the early morning. Chickens are protective of their eggs, which required that I carry my pail of cracked corn when I entered the chicken-house. Scattering a handful of this corn across the floor made most chickens leave their nest. A few with strongest mothering instincts chose to spread their wing feathers outward until they covered their nest. Sitting there, like stern little soldiers, they refused to blink their eyes, giving them a dazed appearance.

I selected one sitting, rigid soldier, the smallest of the group, then inched my soft hand under the chicken's full-feathered skirt. My hand inched closer and closer, nearing her eggs, while I stared into her steely eyes. Her eyes softened the farther I inched, and then suddenly changed from steely to loving. I knew, at this point, she viewed my closed hand as one of her eggs. A bigger than usual egg, I'll grant you, but does anyone know what a chicken thinks? Before she came to her senses, I had her egg. This made her come out of her spell and return to her usual, feisty wits. She gave my hand a few sharp, punishing pecks before deserting her nest for the cracked corn on the floor.

I knew my chickens well for I had been with them since they had hatched. They arrived at our home in early spring as peeps, when still bits of yellow fluff in a cardboard box.

Packed into these boxes were one-hundred peeps. The boxes had holes on the top and sides, about the size of a penny. The holes were for breathing purposes, but we used them as peep holes. We watched as our yellow fluffs moved in waves across the bottom, waves very much like sweeping fields of golden grain. The sounds coming from the box were engaging, soft peeps, which kicked us into nurturing mode.

The peeps were placed in our chicken-house, which was wooden and the size of a cabin. One door and a few windows were on the front of the house, with more windows on the sides. It sat fifty or so feet from the back door of our house. This building existed for the sole purpose of raising peeps to adolescent age. There was one exception, however; my sisters and I used it as our favorite playhouse when the chicks no longer occupied the space.

Upon first opening the box, the chicks seem disoriented. First, one chick, the leader, ran out of the box on the tiniest of feet. Others quickly followed, until the running yellow chicks resembled a stream of melted butter flowing from the box.

Earlier in the day, before the peeps arrived, we had placed feeders and water bowls in the chicken house. One chick now found a feeder and began eating corn mash. Soon, all the other chicks rushed over to eat as well. Baby chicks hatch from their eggs already knowing how to play "follow the leader".

The feeder was simply a quart canning jar that had been screwed onto a metal base fashioned specifically for that purpose. The base had six openings where the chicks crowded and fed. The water bowl was made much the same, with a canning jar screwed onto a metal base. The feed and water released automatically, following gravity's instructions.

When the chicks arrived, they had coats of pure fluff, fluff that should have kept the chicks cozy and warm. But such was not the case. Chicks arrived still in need of warmth from their mothers. We had placed heaters in the chick house before the boxes arrived. These heaters kept the chicks toasty warm for their first few weeks of life.

Although we tried our best to make sure that each chick would grow to pullet size, dangers lurked. Their first danger came from smothering. Chicks bunched together for protection and warmth, and sometimes the smaller, weaker peeps smothered from bunching.

The second danger for chicks was being trampled to death. Chicks, rushed here and there, instead of taking their time. In the rush, they trampled smaller, weaker chicks to death. In the first few weeks, we counted the casualty rate on two hands: one dead chick, two dead chicks, three dead chicks, four, etc.

If a chick survived the early few weeks, the chick would make it to pullet age. Pullet age, actually, was a chick's most dangerous age. Pullets are puberty-aged people. Throughout the summer we had fed, watered, and cared for our chicks. We had watched as yellow fluff became harsh and stiff. By early fall, all fluff was gone, and had been replaced by ugly white and gray bristles. Our chicks were in pullet age, where they would be separated into male and female groups.

A male pullet was in the worst of circumstances, and a weak-looking female couldn't expect to fare better. Both groups were destined to swim in big canning kettles before reaching their first birthday.

One lucky male, however, would be saved from kettle death. The farmer would make the decision. As he carefully looked over his male pullets, the males sensed they were in some sort of contest. They primped and pranced and flashed their brightest tail feathers at the farmer, then crowed their finest calls. The farmer took his time, allowing each male to perform, before making his selection. But, on that very night, a new rooster was crowned king of the chicken house.

But, already a king rooster ruled the chicken house. And, as everyone knows, neither chickens nor people can have two kings at the same time. The old cock somehow sensed the enemy in the camp, and spread his wings, stiffened his legs, and puffed his feathers out until he doubled his size. He intended to fight his new competitor until one was dead, and he didn't think it would be him.

The wise farmer, not wanting an injured cock, grabbed the old bird by his ankles and yanked him out of his flock. He then quickly placed the old rooster's neck between two nails on the chopping block. One swift swipe with his hatchet was all it took to separate head from body.

The farmer presented the headless rooster to his wife, who received it with joy. She swished the huge bird up and down in a bucket of steaming water. She then defrocked him of his royal feathers and roasted him naked for supper.

The farmer had wisely known that keeping two roosters in his hen house would have caused a bloody war. Although the chickens wouldn't have joined in the fight, just watching the melee would have disrupted their egg production.

Strangely enough, however, when the healthy rooster paraded around, up and down, the chickens felt protected and laid many eggs.

As a young girl I wondered about this rooster situation, and asked mother, "What good is one rooster? He doesn't lay eggs. Why aren't all the roosters sold?"

She patiently explained, "Esther May, keeping one rooster keeps our chickens happy. And chickens that are happy lay eggs."

That made sense to me. I knew our rooster was happy, for I heard his joyous crow each morning. And I knew our chickens were happy for they laid many eggs.

The barn troop returned from their farm chores and I returned from my chicken chores about the same time. Breakfast waited on the table, but before one single piece of food could touch our lips, a silent grace was said. Our plates were quickly emptied. We picked them up and licked them clean, not to ease the dishwasher's job, but because we were still hungry and wished we had more.

Leaving the table hungry was part of our frugal pilgrim discipline training. Pilgrims must be toughened to prepare for their hard life, which would surely come their way.

My brothers were toughened further at school. They were teased about their sugar-bowl haircuts; they were teased about their suspenders; and they were teased about their poopy-smelling barn shoes. "No fighting back," mother had instructed. "You must stand there and take it."

Such was the life of a pilgrim. But God, who saw all, witnessed our longsuffering and was very pleased. He kept us, His most favored, in the palm of His hand.

For steadfastly keeping to our narrow pathway, great and bountiful treasures would be ours when we went to heaven. Promises of gold and silver, and precious jewels such as diamonds, emeralds and sapphires, the very riches denied to us upon earth would flow freely into our hands once we arrived in heaven.

Some may believe it strange that we would be denied treasures upon earth, yet could have them in heaven. The answer is simple: The sin of coveting, so prevalent upon earth, will not exist in heaven. Basically, the reason is that folks who covet on earth can't go to heaven. So, with coveting gone, jewels will be allowed.

In the OOM world, individual identity must be sacrificed for the identity of the community. Birthdays came and went without the slightest mention. Christmas was not celebrated with trees dressed in shiny tinsel, colored bulbs and gaudy baubles. All this was of pagan origin, we were told. Halloween couldn't be celebrated either because of its pagan connection. Valentine's Day was connected to some sort of saint, so that was out as well. I never knew who pagans and saints were, but feared them just the same.

Celebrating the Fourth of July was out because that day honored secular government. We were to be a separate and religious people, and to give all our honor and glory to God, who lived everywhere, and to His son Jesus Christ, who lived in heaven. So we didn't celebrate any one or any day here upon earth. We had no parades, picnics or parties, but worked those days instead.

As you might suspect, some of my siblings had a more difficult time walking the narrow pilgrim pathway than others. Obedience was of utmost importance, which meant giving up active control of one's mind and body, and living passively, as those who are controlled must do.

My one sister, Ruth, had an especially difficult time, and insisted that she taste and test and try everything before assigning it to the "sin-and-no-can-do" list. Rebellious was how mother described her. And the best way to get rid of rebellion is to spank it out of a child.

One day my rebellious sister picked up the word "heck" at school, and decided to try it out at the supper table. She liked the way it rolled around on her tongue, so said it again, and louder. The word pleasured her so much that she laughed and said it once more. Clearly, she had ventured into "challenge" territory, which could not be dismissed with a flip of the hand.

My mother promptly forbade my sister to ever say the word again. But my rebellious sister did, and she said it over and over again. Each time she said it, she laughed. Indignant by now, and probably feeling assaulted, mother ordered my heck sister from the table, and demanded she make haste to her bedroom. Heck had no supper that night.

The next day at the supper table, my rebellious sister said "heck" again, and inquired of mother as to why it was wrong. My mother didn't answer, but said she was to be obedient without questioning, and sent my sister to her room without supper again.

On the following morning, when mother awakened her children with her usual call up the stairs, my heck sister didn't appear. After several calls and still no appearance, mother climbed the stairs to check, and found her still in bed.

"Get up!" said Mother.

Ruth made it to her feet, but swayed back and forth, as if ready to faint. Alarmed, Mother put her back into bed, and then rushed to the kitchen, where she made some warm broth. Then, she hurriedly returned to aid my weak sister. Spoonfuls of broth were administered, a little at a time, until my heck sister was able to stand on her feet without swaying.

Pilgrims learned early in life that saying "heck" was forbidden, for that word meant "hell"—a place reserved for the evil, and somehow, if you said it, you were evil, as well. We weren't allowed to say "gosh" either, for that meant God. "Damn" meant you might be damning someone to hell forever. It was not our place to "damn" others, but was something for our Lord God to do.

My childhood training was like growing up in "control" camp. My mother, head warden, was charged with the laborious and overwhelming day-to-day duties of making sure her children were raised properly. Being raised properly had nothing to do with getting good grades in school and bringing home a report card filled with A's. It meant raising sons who would learn the farming duties necessary to carry forward the agrarian way of life, and to be the rooster of his house. It meant raising daughters who would save their beautiful eggs for a proper OOM boy, and be the chicken in his house. It meant having a box filled with fluffy chicks of your own someday.

Perhaps now you will understand why I responded to my friend's question as I did about my cozy childhood. Perhaps you'll understand why I said, "It wasn't cozy at all."

SUBJUGATION

A pilgrim must give up his/her life for the community.

CHAPTER 4

The Adolescent Pilgrim

In the life of a pilgrim, sex is secretive. And where sex is secretive, sneaking thrives like weeds. My earliest sex education was a show-and-tell session, which involved a sneak-and-peek into the plush pasturelands that lay just across the graveled road from our home.

The greatest sneak of all time is recorded in the Bible, in the book of Genesis, to be exact. There, Adam and Eve dwelled in the Garden of Eden, seemingly without care. God told the couple they could eat whatever they pleased, except the *apple* from the Tree of Knowledge.

One day while God attended other matters, Adam and Eve ate some of the forbidden apple. Immediately, they saw they were naked, and stuck a fig leaf here, a few leaves there. When God returned and saw the fig leaves, He knew what they had done. He was not pleased and shooed them from the Garden of Eden.

In the pilgrim family, great effort is placed on the evils of nudity. Boys and girls have separate outhouses, separate bedrooms, and take separate baths in the darkness of the basement.

Nudity extends to *same* sex as well. Although my sisters and I slept together in the same bedroom, two of us to a bed, and two beds in the room, the four of us never undressed in front of each other. Instead, we undressed in the privacy of our closet.

My heck sister saw this nudity obsession as an "apple" that needed plucked. One afternoon, while our mother took a needed nap, "heck" led her younger siblings into our Garden of Eden.

74

Barefooted, our soles hardened from months of going shoeless, three girls in cotton dresses and three boys in bibbed overalls easily skipped across the graveled road. There, we encountered our first obstacle, an electric, barbed-wire fence, the kind that penned cows in, the kind that penned the bull out—the bull we nicknamed "Awful" who dwelled in these plush pastureland from time to time—just to keep the cows happy, as mother had said.

Trained by the bull, we slithered under the fence, slithered as fast as a snake. The thought of Awful's steamy behavior filled us with fear and made our hearts flutter, made us pause and look around, look around like a Meerkat.

Surprisingly, Awful wasn't there; yet happy cows were everywhere, which made me wonder how much Mother really knew.

First, we passed an old elm where chickadees had perched on tree branches. They chirped: "Chickadee! Chickadee!"—which pleased us so much that we chirped our names back, twice, as they had for us. I said, "Esther Esther"—my youngest brother said, "Paul Paul"—and my sister Ruth said, "Heck Heck"—quite loudly, with no fear of missing her supper.

Heck then led us up a small hill to where a sprinkling of oak trees made their home. We climbed under the branches, grateful for the shade, grateful for the rest. Unfortunately, rest and relaxation were words my heck sister never learned. She quickly had us up and about, and looking for a stick. It couldn't be one stick for all six of us, but had to be six sticks in total, each having their own. And, it couldn't be just any old stick either, but had to be a perfect stick.

"The perfect stick," she exclaimed, "must be skinny, no branches, like a stick you would use to stir a pot." We did as she said, for she was our older sibling. And we knew the importance of obeying elders.

After finding our perfect sticks, things unfolded rather quickly. We sniffed the air, as someone does when realizing *stuff* is not up to *snuff*. And, truly, it wasn't, for Heck then pulled up her skirt and pushed down her panty, and exposed herself to us, to the trees, to the grass, to the sun, for heaven's sake, to all! She instructed her siblings to do likewise. Naturally, with no skirt to pull up, my brothers had to drop their pants.

What to do? What to do? The question jumbled our brains. Mama would be so mad if we followed Heck's commands. Horror would distort her pretty face! And punishments would proceed—punishments for all.

Fearfully, we looked around in all directions, just in case Mama had followed. Adam and Eve must have behaved similarly, and searched to make sure God wasn't nearby before plucking the apple in the Garden. But He wasn't around, so they chose for themselves. And Mama wasn't around, so we did the same.

We chose the evil path. Well, actually it turned out to be the good path. That's how life tricks you sometimes. You go down an evil path with hearts all aflutter, and it turns out to be the good path after all.

I can tell you this: We had a most illuminating lesson in how to tell the difference between a girl and a boy, a very illuminating lesson, indeed. It seems to me that learning these differences is as necessary for one's educational growth as learning that one plus two equals three, and as necessary as knowing that two cups make one pint.

It's these bits of knowledge that add up when you're young. Knowledge elevates your feet, which enables you to walk higher through your teens, and enables you to touch the sky in your twenties. Carrying one's head higher is so essential for a pilgrim girl, so essential for all girls and boys, I would say!

Still, we had the sticks, which appeared dead upon the ground. But Moses—my heck sister in this case—picked up hers and it came to life.

First, she urinated and defecated upon a patch of grass, deposited—you might say, as cows deposit in the pasture. She then took her stick and stirred her deposit, and instructed us to do likewise.

If my heck sister's intention was to teach us how cow pies were made, I simply didn't want to know. Would this bit of knowledge do me one bit of good in my teens and in my twenties? I couldn't possibly believe so.

But, overall, my show-and-tell lesson, which turned out to be more show than tell, was generous and immense. And the apple Heck plucked off the tree of knowledge that day was large enough to last me for a lifetime.

Yet, what we learned paled in comparison to what Adam and Eve learned on their day. The apple they ate enabled them to discern good from evil, which they passed along in their genes to all future generations. Now, that was some apple!

An equally informative sex education lesson, although not of show-and-tell type, came from my first cousins. These girls said things together, as if they were one. "All is not peaches and cream when you get married," they said together. "All is not peaches at all."

Proceeding in one voice, they further said: "When you get married, your husband will want to put his *thing* into you. You won't like it! You won't like it at all! But you have to let him do it, 'cause that's the only way you can get a baby. And a baby is what we want!" They paused for a moment, sighed deeply, then said in a voice that sounded more like a wail: "A baby is all we want!"

Granted, these particular first cousins were of "Chicken Little" variety—those who live their life as if the sky is falling. But it gave me my first clue as to why mother insisted that her daughters keep their skirts down and their knees pressed tightly together.

Generally, an Old Order Mennonite girl receives little sex education before she enters her wedding bed, which places her in an inferior and submissive position. Her husband, on the other hand, comes with some knowledge. Some of his education comes from watching farm animals do their thing. And some may have come from practical experience. Oh, not experience with any good OOM girl, for we have our knees pressed tightly together, but experience from a visit to a whorehouse or two before he enters the wedding bed.

Just when I thought my sex education was complete, a couple of the community's Old Maids knocked on our front door. Although a warm July day, these women wore their typical Old Order Mennonite garb—their black wide-brimmed bonnets tied neatly under their chins—their dresses, dark and collarless, with long skirts that sashayed across the tops of their black shoe laces as they walked.

After usual greetings were exchanged, one Maid said, "On Saturday, we plan to sell our extra produce in Youngstown." The other inquired if heck sister and I might come along.

Upon hearing the words *making money* and *working* in the same sentence, mother's ears grew to jackrabbit size. "Indeed, they can," replied mother, her voice sing-song-y with joy. "We have excess produce as well, which I was going to have to can within the week. But now selling . . . oh, selling is such a better idea."

On Saturday morning, Heck and I arose early and went into the garden. Soon we had baskets filled with freshly-picked peas, lettuce, tomatoes and green beans. Within a short time, the Old Maids came along—wearing their typical garb—and motoring a rather new Ford, which had been painted totally black, the only sort of car allowed by the church.

It took about an hour to reach Youngstown's tenement city, where a forest of apartment buildings occupied block after block. Being new to the area, Heck and I were soon lost in the wilderness of buildings. We looked this way and that, which sent our long braids a-bobbing. The Old Maids, meanwhile, guided by memory, quickly found a place to park.

We took our filled baskets and walked down long hallways, knocking on apartment doors. Black people lived in these buildings. Our mother had taught us that blackness was only skin deep—and that on the inside, black people were the same as us. We didn't even think of them as being different.

"Would you like to buy some?" we asked the apartment dweller, our eyes looking at the floor. It wasn't our custom to speak to strangers, and we were shy about asking others to do something for us.

The apartment dwellers, however, showered us with praises. "What cute little braids," they exclaimed, "and look at your dresses. Have you ever seen anything made so nicely?" They even liked our black stockings, which we hated. All this noticing made us grow four inches in the one hour we were there.

They readily purchased our fresh vegetables, which they claimed were at such nominal prices. Because they purchased plenty, we finished earlier than planned, and returned to the car.

Before getting in, the Old Maids chatted off to the side, then returned and suggested, well, giggled, that we'd visit the nearby Sears and Roebuck's department store before heading for home.

Soon the two Old Maids, with my heck sister and I traipsing closely behind, hurried down one aisle and up another. The Maids walked as if on a mission, passing the toy section, the kitchenware section, the dress section, up one aisle, down another, up-and-down, up-and-down, all in haste. Finally, they slowed, and talked with each other, then made a quick left into the lingerie department.

Once there, they scurried to the counter displaying bras. Such items displayed there! Heck and I averted our eyes, believing such clothing worldly and of the devil. We looked up to the ceiling, then down to the floor, up and down, back and forth, trying our best to not glimpse at anything that would displease God. But the excess giggling coming from the Old Maids' location made us look their way. Each held a lacy bra up to her chest, each swishing her bra up and down, up and down. Swish! Swish! Swish! Swish!—laughing and giggling, laughing and giggling—as if in great pleasure, which made us think: UGH!

Then one Maid composed herself enough to manage a question: "Can you imagine anyone needing these?" This made the other Maid double over in laughter. "I can't! I can't!" she exclaimed, her eyes swimming in tears of mirth.

My heck sister and I did not find this funny. We did not find this funny at all! Yet, captured as we were, what could we do but watch as this horror scene played out again and again. Throughout our ordeal, the Old Maids frequently glanced our way, just to make sure we were still watching. This wasn't educational and this wasn't entertaining, yet, curiously and confusingly, it made our *places* tingle, places we didn't even know we had until then.

Embarrassed, we crept into another aisle and hid behind wooden counters. The Old Maids found this even more amusing, and sought us out. There, they jiggled the bras they had brought along with them, up and down, across their chest, jiggling and giggling, jiggling and giggling, until they tired of their weird activity. Then they drove us home.

Since anything that had to do with sex in our home was treated as if it was an FBI highest-level secret, we treated our experience with tightly buttoned lips. When our mother asked, "Did you sell all the produce?" we answered, "Yes, yes we did,"—and held out our hands and showed her the money we had earned that afternoon. We then gave the coins to our mother, as required.

Life tricks you at times. The embarrassing afternoon I had spent with the Old Maids turned out to be good for me, after all. Countless objects I had previously overlooked now stood out as big as mountains before my very eyes.

For instance, I now noticed that mother's one-piece corselet had a bra top. Although different from the bras the old maids dangled before us, it was a bra top, nonetheless. I could see that clearly now! This corselet appeared in the laundry from time to time, and I had touched it and felt it. It was heavy and coarse when wet, and required quite a struggle just to put it through the wringer. And then a bigger struggle ensued just to drag this corselet to the clothesline and pin it up.

I asked mother once why she wore this corselet. She said, "It's because I have so many children, I have to wear **something** to keep my organs in place." Wow! Talk about being a martyr! She may have been a martyr but she also was a master of combining an explanation, an exclamation, and a complaint into one sentence, which, definitely, came from having so many children, I'm sure.

At another time I found an unusual box hiding on the highest shelf in our fruit cellar. I had to stack two crates together just to reach this shelf, but it was well worth the trouble. The box was gray and worn, as if it had been opened many times. The box indicated that it contained a breast pump. *A breast pump—hmmm. What could that be?* I puzzled. I slowly opened the box, afraid of what might be lurking inside. Oddly, inside was a funnel attached to a rubber pump, which I squeezed, just to see what it would do. It created a picture of a cow pump in my brain. Disgustedly, I quickly put the contraption away and returned the box to the shelf.

I never told mother what I had found, for we discussed nothing about my body that wasn't clothed. All this meant that we discussed my face, my hands, and my feet, but nothing else.

Cultures have rites of passage that prepare young people for dating and marriage. The Apache Indians are known for their Sunrise ceremony; Old Order Mennonites are known for their Singings. Both might be described as a "coming-out" party for young people, but similarities stop abruptly and completely there. Singings are most modest and stoic affairs.

As OOM boys and girls entered their teens, shame about their changing bodies made them bashful and timid around each other. They bundled up with loose clothing to flatten new bumps and hide emergence of curves. Nevertheless, they could be seen, somehow, for it was exactly these bumps and curves that earned them an invitation to attend a Singing.

Singings provided a comfortable opportunity for our teens to mix with one another. How strange for our teens to be uncomfortable with the opposite sex when they had all those brothers and sisters! Yet, such is true. Being comfortable with a sibling isn't the same as being comfortable with someone you might have sex with, after marriage, that is, if all went well.

In our community, Singings took place on a Sunday evening. And, as the name implies, hymns were sung at Singings. But cookies and Kool-Aid were served as well. Games were played to break down awkwardness and timidity. I'm unable to tell you if these games were leftovers from the past. However, in my fifty-plus years in the World, I have never seen them played anywhere other than at Singings. "Drop the Hanky" was one such game. "Taking your Picture with a Spoon" was another.

*   *   *

In "Drop the Hanky"—the teen group formed a large circle, with everyone facing inward. A girl was chosen to stroll along the outside of the circle. She then dropped a hanky behind the feet of a boy she wanted to date. As soon as she dropped the hanky, she took off running around the outside of the circle and tried to get back into his spot. It was vacant now, because the chosen boy had picked up the hanky and was running in the opposite direction, trying his best to beat her back to his spot before she arrived.

When I played "Drop the Hanky" in my teens, I found it to be fun and of great sport. The intended result was to breakdown the awkwardness between girls and boys, and it worked nicely. Best of all, if a girl dropped the hanky behind her special interest's ankle, he was likely to take her home from the Singing.

*   *   *

"Taking Your Picture with a Spoon" was great spoofing fun. This game was rather odd for teenagers who believed that having your picture taken was wrong. However, the game falls into the category of practical joking.

In "Taking Your Picture with a Spoon", the group sat in a circle. An inexperienced newcomer (we'll name Samuel for the sake of simplicity) was asked to leave the room. An experienced player, we'll call Ben, was chosen to be the leader.

Ben took a spoon, and pointed the bowl toward a seated player's face, who we'll call Mary. Ben pretended to photograph Mary.

Samuel (inexperienced) was invited back into the room and tried to guess who had their picture taken. All his guesses were incorrect, which produced great laughter. Finally, Samuel gave up trying to guess, and Mary confessed it was she.

A second player, we'll name Peter, was asked to leave the room. Peter was an experienced player. The spoon-photo was taken again. When Peter was asked to return to the room, and to guess who had their photo taken, Peter answered correctly on the first try. Samuel scratched his head, trying to figure all this out, which produced great laughter within the room.

More successful rounds of the game were played. Samuel (the inexperienced player), finally thought he had learned the secret of the game, and asked to try again. He left the room, returned, and tried guessing. He failed a second time.

Again, an experienced player would leave the room, return, and answer correctly on the first try.

Samuel, confident he finally knew the key to the game, asked to try again. And Samuel failed again. The secret was then revealed.

In the first example, Ben, the leader, had mimicked the actions of Mary. If Mary wiped her brow, Ben wiped his brow. If Mary scratched her ear, Ben scratched his ear. When Mary combed her hair with her fingers, Ben combed his. Anyone who knew this game would catch on immediately, but a newcomer would have trouble connecting the two players, especially if they sat on opposite sides of the circle.

*   *   *

At the end of a Singing, a teenage boy might ask a girl if he could take her home. If she agreed, once at her home, the couple sat in the parlor and visited, where they were left alone. Other family members snored away in their bedrooms, confident that nothing sexual or inappropriate would take place. Besides, they needed their sleep, for early-morning chores required early-morning awakenings. A cow that needing milked is not a patient cow, and has no qualms about "mooing" as loudly as a coyote howls.

The girl, now with her boyfriend captured in her parlor, knew the way to her young lad's heart. Earlier in the day she had baked scrumptious Snicker Doodle cookies, just in case she had a suitor.

In dating times, secrets ruled the day, progressing as if no one knew the couple was seeing each other. Yet it was a secret known by everyone throughout the community. The secret evoked snickers and grins, but not words. When the couple became engaged, no one spoke of this either. The secret was only revealed a week before the wedding, when the couple announced at Sunday morning worship service their intent to marry.

Old Order Mennonites require that you be a church member before you are allowed to marry. Since teens usually joined the church before they began to date, this was easily accommodated.

However, although extremely rare, if a young OOM girl found herself pregnant before joining the church, a quick baptism and membership was arranged. The same would be true if her suitor had not joined the church yet. After joining the church, the couple would have to confess before the congregation at Sunday morning church service. All they needed to say was, "We put our cart before the horse and we'll never do it again." All was forgiven and a quick marriage ensued.

A different situation was encountered if a young Old Order Mennonite girl found herself pregnant due to a relationship with a non-Old Order Mennonite boy. In my realm of familiarity, a young girl who found herself in such a circumstance was quickly whisked off to her family doctor. With her mother at her side, the girl walked into the doctor's office in pregnant condition, and returned home pregnant-less. Most sorrowful, the girl might return home in a sterile condition.

The community's women, as part of their regular life, frequently visited one another in the morning. Since these visits were always unannounced, mother viewed them as spying opportunities. She claimed their real purpose was to make sure she was raising her children in the proper OOM way, which meant making sure her daughters had their hair severely parted in the middle, and making sure her daughters were wearing the mandatory long, cotton, black stockings. She could have been right about the spying, for these ladies had eyes that darted everywhere. When these women arrived, even innocent little dust balls ran for the corners, just to keep safe from being spotted by their probing eyes.

As the years passed, these visits changed in nature, and became obvious scouting expeditions. Unbeknownst to their sons, who would have howled out with embarrassing protestations, their mothers checked the community girls for potential marriage material. When a possible match was made, a flurry of get-togethers was arranged between the two families, all designed to place the young girl and boy in close proximity. Carefully observing, with their hands clasped together, mothers noted all exchanges that could be identified as "sparks". One or two of these sparks would be enough to relax their clasped hands. Successful interactions meant more meetings must be arranged, and with haste.

My check-out happened when I had barely reached my teens, and without my slightest awareness, for I was still trying to process my periods and my need for them. But what happened then, even I couldn't ignore, for it involved clicking sounds emitted from one of the mothers. I had never heard such sounds coming from a human before. Quickly following her clicking was her comment, "Look at her cute dimple! How many girls have that!" She pointed to my face and repeated: "She has a dimple."

"Yes, a cute dimple, for sure," said the second mother, "but if you ask me, she's a bit stocky. See this!" She pinched my waist and ended up with two inches of fat, which made her roll up her nose.

Stocky came as no surprise to me, for I thought of myself as a little plump. *So what? I thought!* It was not a big deal as far as I was concerned. In the first place, I rarely saw my plumpness, for pilgrim houses are scarce in mirrors. But once I was told that I had a "cute" dimple, I ran for the small mirror that hung above the wash basin in the kitchen. And there it was, for sure. I had a dimple.

Telling me that I had a dimple was like putting a candle inside me. I glowed with this knowledge. Yet, in case someone thought I was prideful, I kept it to myself. Retaining my modest pilgrim-girl image with a candle glowing inside was not easy. It was not easy to do, at all.

But best of all, this meant I would marry someday. And, I would have many children!

Sadly, not all of my siblings were as fortunate. In our religion, one child, sometimes two or more, was held back to care for their parents as they aged. People of the world have Social Security benefits and Medicare, and a host of other programs to assist their elderly. But we had none of these, for our religion labeled such social programs as secular, and refused to use them. "It was wrong," we were told, "to yoke yourself with secular governments of this world."

Denied the possibility of marriage, two of my siblings were groomed to take care of our elderly parents. These siblings were my sister Sarah and my brother Paul.

As children, we were taught to keep modesty as a backdrop in our life, and part of this image was wearing the simple dress. Although the different dress was designed to reflect our unpretentious and humble spirit, it actually made us stand out in the real world.

We were also taught that our different dress served as our testimony. People of the world would see our plain dress and know that we were the true children of God. If they followed our way, they would go to heaven, too. All this testimony would take place without the need to say a single word. As such, we became passive evangelists.

In the first episode of the 2004 *Amish in the City*[6] television show, a most dramatic example of "dressing differently" takes place. This reality show was filmed in the big city of Los Angeles, CA. The City represented the World. Into this World were brought four Amish and four City Dwellers, who would share a Hollywood mansion for a specified period of time.

I was immediately drawn into this show, for the two teenaged Amish girls, Naomi and Ruth, were around seventeen, the same age as I when leaving the OOM community. They, too, had grown up in the Northeastern Ohio farm country. With such highly-relatable circumstances, I anxiously awaited each episode, eager to learn how these girls dealt with their move from the Past into the Present.

Nearly ten years has passed since this reality show aired, yet much information can be garnered from a quick "Amish in the City" Google or Yahoo search. Actual recordings play full episodes.

Episode One: The Amish, two girls and three boys, dressed in their traditional clothing, arrived at the big Los Angeles mansion. This mansion was their home for the duration of the show. Sharing this large home with the Amish were the five City Dwellers: the teens of the world.

On their first day, the City Dwellers took the Amish shopping for store-bought modern clothing. For the Amish, this purchase was a novel experience, for their clothing had always been homemade.

A visit to a theme park was planned for the following day. The Amish and the City Dwellers switched clothing for this occasion: the Amish wearing modern—and the City Dwellers wearing Amish.

The City Dwellers immediately noticed that others in the park viewed them differently. They felt that the glances and stares sent their way were full of disdain. The experience left them confused and hurt. After all, they were the same City Dweller teenagers they had been the day before, yet people, now, obviously, judged them to be "less"—simply because of their dress, They experienced shame; they wanted to hide. Above all, they wanted their day to end quickly so they could change back into their worldly garments.

The Amish, meanwhile, wearing modern clothing, enjoyed their day. They giddily strutted around the theme park and tried every ride. They interacted with entertainers, twirling with them in dance numbers. They sampled all food and laughed gleefully through it all. At the end of the day, fortunately, the Amish didn't have to return their modern garments, but were told they could keep them for the week they'd be in the City.

Who would have guessed that dressing differently would have taken such a toll on one's self-esteem? Who could have guessed that clothing could make such a difference in how one is viewed and judged? Who could have guessed that it could make such a difference in how one interacts with another? Who could have guessed that different dress would so easily keep members of their community from mingling with the world?

Two major behaviors emerge from this exchange of clothing. Both highlight the intended result of isolation.

(1) People of the world view people who dress differently with trepidation—and are unlikely to approach them.
(2) People who dress differently notice the looks of uneasiness they receive from people of the world—and are unlikely to interact with them.

As a child who experienced the shame of dressing differently, I found that such embarrassment transferred into internal pain. The following are some of the results:

(1) Energy, when focused on nursing internal pain, leaves little energy for compassion of others.
(2) Energy, when focused on nursing internal pain, scatters attention, and leaves little energy available for learning.

In my childhood community, strict "all-the-same" patterns were used for constructing garments, but individuality was allowed in the selection of fabrics. The women wore pastel colors and fabrics designed with geometrics, dots, and little flowers. While one woman chose tiny green tree leaves on pale pink, a second chose tiny winding yellow roses on willow green. A third chose a simple black geometric pattern on violet.

It was different with the Amish, however, for they wore only plain-colored fabrics, usually blue or black, with no flowers or geometric patterns. Neither OOM nor Amish girls or women are allowed to wear fabrics of bold and ostentatious colors. An example would be red, which was not allowed in either religion.

Dressing all the same has great economic value. Material purchased in huge bolts is definitely cheaper.

"What you wear tells who you are!" mother often said. The OOM dress reflected modesty, humility, and passivity.

A member's identity shows up best through work. A woman may be known as baking the best pies; her husband may be known as raising the most productive milk cows; and her brother may shine through his excellent crafts and woodworking skills.

Children strive for individual identity, as well. My sister Ruth, better known as my heck sister in this book, achieved identity for her neatness. When ironing clothes, she carefully pressed out every crease and wrinkle.

Our younger brothers were the only boys in our community that wore ironed overalls, the legs on them perfectly creased in the center.

My sister Grace shone in the kitchen, her scrumptious cookies and cakes made her quite popular with her siblings.

A young boy may have a knack for getting more milk out of a cow than does his father and brothers. A second boy might plow a field in record speed, his rows straighter than any other community member.

Since a humble disposition is prized above all, praise is not given for accomplishing superior work. A nod might be all you'll receive, but a nod is enough to make a pilgrim's heart leap.

Individual identity will **not** be seen in the coverings and caps worn by the Amish and the Old Order Mennonite girls and women. Amish young girls generally wear caps, but this is rare for an OOM girl. Both groups, however, wear the covering when they join the church, which occurs in their mid-to-late teens. Covering fabrics vary, but generally are of sheer, white organdy or white mesh.

The general consensus regarding the wearing of the covering is that it reflects the modesty and submissiveness of the OOM woman. My mother and aunts, when queried as to why they wore the head covering, answered, "We like to have our head covered. It's God's will that we do so. We don't mind wearing them at all."

Such quick, identical responses bore witness that they were part of the "rote learning" that took place in our highly-controlled community. We learned how to answer outsiders' questions.

A nun's habit shows who she is; a priest's collar shows who he is; a king's cloak and crown shows who he is; a prisoner's uniform shows who he is; a man's business suit shows who he is; and a woman's mandatory head-covering shows who she is.

A trip into OOM and Amish communities will reveal many differences in coverings, which might baffle outsiders. In some communities, women will tuck their covering strings into their dress bodice; in other communities, women will casually toss the strings across their shoulders and allow them to flow loosely upon their backs. Some covering strings are black and some are white.

The conformity of women's coverings—the color, the design, the peculiarities of the strings—all highly visible, might seem without rationale, but such is not the case. Coverings serve as community identifiers, and provide information as to who is a member of which group of people (community).

All aspects of the covering are under the control of the bishop, the man who has highest control in the Old Order Mennonite religion. Each bishop rules a particular district, and oversees a group of churches. Each church has a preacher and deacon.

Bishops and preachers are chosen by God in a procedure called lots, which was used in the Bible. Bishops serve for life, and have absolute power over the community. They determine how a woman wears her covering strings, for example, and how a man wears his beard.

The official reason given for the head covering comes from a Biblical Passage: I Corinthians 11:3-7. Old Order Mennonites use only the King James Version of the Bible, claiming it is the true Bible. Paul, the Apostle instructed that the man of every family is the head, and must pray or prophesy with his head uncovered. A woman, however, must pray with her head covered. If it had been Paula, the Apostle, all might have been different.

Great utilitarian value can be found in the wearing of a head covering. Two such values are:

(1) Wearing a head covering means you can have a bad hair day and no one knows or cares.
(2) Wearing a head covering means you no longer have to bother scheduling that once-a-month visit to the hairdresser.

If the construction and design of the covering was under the control of women, undoubtedly, quilting get-togethers would be lively affairs. Comments such as this certainly would be heard: "I'm tired of wearing strings on my covering," voiced Martha. "They get into my soup some times. Why don't we go string-less?"

And, surely, the women would take cues from the colorful flowers in their gardens. Sometimes we'd see pink strings—at other times, blue—at other times purple, or one orange and one yellow. Colorful covering strings would pop up everywhere.

We had good dresses, which we wore to school and church. We had faded and worn dresses, which we called our everyday dresses. Our everyday dresses bore a few patches here and there, and generally had a fade-line around the skirt bottom due to lengthening, a time or two or three, as it passed from older sisters to younger sisters. Our sleeves bore witness to having been lengthened a time or two also. A dress had to be threadbare before being assigned to a rag box. A dress in a rag box might be rescued a time or two, as well, at a time when needed. Then, the best of the material was cut out and sewn into a baby gown for a new arrival due in the family any day. The newborn loved its softness, and perhaps it's lovely smell, having been soaked in laughter, sweat and tears by the many girl members of the family.

As a treat from mending, Mother allowed us to embroider samplers, or embroider a tiny flower or bird at the corner of our handkerchief.

At other times we cut squares, triangles and rectangles from our scrap-bag materials. When dresses were cut out, scraps were placed in bags to be pieced together at a later date. This sort of quilt was called a "scrap quilt"—for obvious reasons. Our quilts were used for functional purposes only. We never thought of them as ornamental bed coverings, or ever hung them on a wall. Since our stitches were as disciplined (tiny and intricate) as we were, our quilts lasted several lifetimes.

The material used to make quilts reflected the material allowed in our dresses. Since we used calico, cotton material with different colors and designs, our quilts were made of such material, as well. Since the Amish wear solid colors, generally of blue or black or purple, their quilts will be made with such fabrics.

Others, who are closer to the many Amish and Mennonite communities, remind me that these differences may not exist in quilts that are made more recently. The Amish and Old Order Mennonite women, quite astute in knowing the laws of supply and demand, now use various fabrics to sew into quilts, I am told. And the fabrics may not reflect what they wear in their own dresses.

In my growing-up days, manual work began before dawn and ended after dusk. If I dared voice a complaint, Mother said, "People on this earth are supposed to work. You'll have plenty of time for rest after you die and go to heaven." My mother was a good-pilgrim example. To help her get through her day, she sang beautiful valium-filled hymns.

We were not allowed to use musical instruments, which were classified as too worldly by the church. Yet, mother's pure voice struck each note as beautifully and as tone-perfect as any string plucked on the finest violin. Some of her favorites were about the sweet by-and-by, and how joyous it would be when death finally came. At that time, we would have a wonderful reunion with those who had passed on before, the hymn informed. These hymns emphasized the passive nature of pilgrim life. Sure, life on earth would be hard, but stop your grumbling! How joyous heaven would be, your eternal reward. Knowing that my father and mother and my sisters and brothers would all be there kept my feet planted firmly upon my pilgrim pathway.

Other hymns were about the need to toil through the morning hours, noon, and evening hours, *'til day was done,* as the song said.

Many hymns were love songs to God and Jesus. "Oh How I Love Jesus" was a song I remember well.

Sometimes mother tailored her song to the task. *Onward Christian Soldiers* became her favorite when it was time for me to set the supper table. She belted forth this song in drumbeat fashion, which set my feet to marching. Jauntily, I tramped around the kitchen table, assigning ten plates, ten cups, and ten teaspoons to their proper supper stations. Soon serving dishes of tasty, steamy food filled the air with mouthwatering aromas. They were lined up in the bare center of the table, as eight hungry children filed onto the two long benches on opposite sides of the table.

Papa and Mama took a chair at one end. Papa would be at the head, then Mama next, and then her youngest child. Progressing up the benches would be the second youngest, etc., with the oldest children on the end farthest from Mama and Papa. A silent grace was said by Papa before we were allowed one taste of food. Since it was silent, who knew what was said except God in heaven, who hears all, whether silent or spoken.

ISOLATION

Walking in the narrow way makes you think in the
narrow way.

CHAPTER 5

The Uneducated Pilgrim

In the previous chapter I described a great sneak, one most joyful in nature, and one that would have made even Adam and Eve blush. The sneak, a show-and-tell sex lesson of epic proportions, provided my siblings and me with information that seemed rightfully ours. For aren't our sexual organs necessary for procreation? Aren't they as necessary as our fingers and our toes and our tongue and our nose? Aren't they as necessary as our head and our heart? Why was such information withheld from us? Perhaps this chapter, which is about our greatest grief, will shed light on this massive dilemma.

As I write this chapter, I am reading Stephen King's latest book *11/22/63*. The protagonist in King's story is a school teacher named Jake Epping.

To make a few extra dollars, Jake took a second job. On Saturday mornings he taught GED students—students who had wished to graduate from high school and had been unable to do so, for various reasons.

Jake gave his class an assignment. "Write a story about something that changed your life," he instructed.

When Jake graded his students' papers, he noticed many grammatical and spelling errors. Nonetheless, he graded one paper with a red A. Then, after thinking more about the story, he added a red plus mark. Jake gave this student an A plus. King explained that the student's story had evoked a response within him. And, according to King, any story that evoked a response deserved an A-plus.

Reading the letters *G E D* evoked a huge response within me, thank you Stephen King. In fact, I cried. I cried for my older siblings who had to take GED courses when in their sixties.

These siblings could rightfully entitle their story: *We flunked because our religion made us do it!* They could then write about how they loved school, attained good grades, yet failed because they were forced to miss too many days. They could tell you that our religion's rules required that they quit school in eighth grade. They could tell you how difficult life is when you have a limited education. Surely, each of their stories would rate a red A-plus. Surely, each would!

Old Order Mennonites are a group of religious people who live in the past. As such, they believe in limiting education according to the needs of the people who lived in the past. If fact, if you asked Old Order Mennonites why their children can't attend school beyond the eighth-grade, all would say, "By the eighth grade, our boys can learn as much as they need to be farmers and carpenters. And our girls can learn as much as they need to be housewives and mothers. There is no need for a higher education."

And, as if to seal off any further discussion, all would then emphatically add: "Going further in school makes one proud, and makes one think they're smart. Only God is smart and knows all. We are to be humble pilgrims."

These excuses reflect another time when eighth-grade education was adequate and served children well. Children, in that day, grew up to be farmers, homemakers, and peasants who worked the fields, and maids and servants who worked for the wealthy. In fact, an eighth-grade education was better than most people could expect. But such is **not** true today!

Timing is everything in the life of an individual—in the life of a family. In our family, my four older siblings were denied a high-school education, while I and my three younger siblings earned our diploma. It wasn't because the younger were smarter than the older—or more diligent—or more attentive—or anything that could reflect upon intelligence or character. It was simply because of timing.

Timing meant my four older siblings attended the one-room schoolhouse that served our OOM community. I and my three younger brothers never attended this school, for, in 1943, the year I was six and scheduled to attend, State Educational Officials closed this school.

Timing meant that, when this one-room school served our community, there was no controversy in honoring our religion's requirement. In fact, the school had only eight grades.

Children were routinely kept home to help with the planting of crops in the spring and the harvesting of crops in the fall. Every Monday, girls were kept home to assist their mothers with the huge family laundry. And boys were kept home during the butchering of farm animals, which happened every October/November.

Education was secondary to working, and no one failed because of missed days in an Old Order Mennonite school.

All this changed when our one-room schoolhouse was closed. Then, my older siblings and I began attending public school—and controversy raised its ugly head. According to state rules, we were no longer permitted to quit school in the eighth grade, but had to attend until sixteen. If we needed to miss school to help plant the corn or hang up the laundry, a parent must request a work permit. These permits, filled out by parents, were approved by our teacher or our school principal.

Ah, what to do? What to do? We had to quit school in eighth grade. But the State of Ohio said we had to go to school until sixteen. What was an Old Order Mennonite to do?

Really, why this dilemma? Why not just quit school at sixteen, and skip all this eighth-grade fuss? Surely the bishops could have been more flexible.

Work permits were issued to accommodate those times when arable-land workers (children in our case) had to help on the farm. At other times, they were issued when children were needed to help out in the home. Surprisingly, work permits were easy for mother to obtain. She simply wrote a note stating she needed extra help, and cited our father's multiple sclerosis condition as her reason.

Work permit requests required that my oldest brother, Mark, be frequently kept home from school for farm-work duties. My older sisters fared no better. In addition to helping our mother with Monday's laundry, they were kept home to can fruits and vegetables in the fall.

Our classmates were no longer OOM; our needs were different from those of other students. Frequent absenteeism left my siblings limping scholastically behind their classmates. And they failed.

When my oldest brother Mark was thirteen, my father's illness worsened to the point where he could no longer do farm work. My mother wrote a note to school, requesting permission that Mark be allowed to quit school. The school approved her request.

But Mark, an extremely intelligent lad, had his IQ measured later in life. His high scores earned him an invitation to join Mensa. If he could have continued his education, who knows what he could have done with his life.

While it was true that mother needed the help of my older siblings, it was also true that she needed to keep them home from school so they could fail. If mother had been honest, she would have written the following:

> *I am keeping my children out of school because I can't allow them to go beyond the eighth grade. I want them to fail. In fact, they must fail two years if I am to faithfully obey the requirements of my religion. All would have been good if they still attended the one-room schoolhouse that served our religion. But, now, in public school, you require my children to attend until sixteen. This means the tenth grade, and my children must quit in the eighth grade. Since your requirements differ from those of my religion, I will follow the rules of my religion.*

With frequent work permits, my four older siblings failed. They were well on their way of meeting the school's requirement (age sixteen) and the religion's requirement (eighth grade). The burden soon shifted onto my shoulders, and onto the shoulders of my three younger siblings, Frank, John and Paul. Even though we attended a good public school, we were encouraged by mother to get bad grades. Failing grades met with approval at home; good grades brought punishment.

What hope did I have of ever getting a good education? I would say none! However, at the tender age of thirteen, I challenged myself with these words: *If you ever want to make something out of yourself in this world, you'll have to do it yourself.* My teachers were responsible for sparking such a realization within me.

To mother's credit, she encouraged me to have a good character, as evidenced in what she wrote in my autograph book. I was fourteen when she wrote the following verse:

> *<u>Who</u> ever you are, be noble.*
> *<u>What</u> ever you do, do well.*
> *<u>When</u> ever you speak, speak kindly.*
> *Give joy <u>where</u> ever you dwell.*

I've underlined the five words in this little verse that are essential to the writer. Well, I've underlined four, but the fifth word—why—is present as well.

Since I had not failed by sixth grade, mother fretted continuously. "Time is running out," she said, and decided to do something about it. She wrote an excuse to the school, stating I was needed to help out at home because of my father's deteriorating condition. The school approved the excuse. She kept me home from February until the end of the school term. Naturally, I flunked. (I know the word is failed but I am using flunked because it hurt like a flunk!)

My three younger brothers, realizing they had to fail twice, purposely performed poorly in school. Their teachers said nothing, for they knew our home situation, and they knew the OOM's position on education.

Timing is everything! Our move to Akron in 1955 negated our need to flunk, but did nothing to elevate our financial situation. My four older siblings, who were in their late teens and early twenties, immediately took jobs to meet our family's living expenses. I and my three younger siblings, while allowed to continue our education, took part-time jobs to help with our family's expenses, as well.

Timing is everything in life. For instance, when I attended Columbiana Public grade school, our classroom day began with the reciting of the "Pledge of Allegiance". My Old Order Mennonite religion forbade that we participate in this ceremony. "When your classmates stand, you are to remain seated," our mother counseled. "We are not citizens of this world. We are citizens of heaven."

A few years ago, I met Richard E. Kelly, author of *Growing up in Mama's Club*, and his recently released book, *The Ghosts from Mama's Club*. Mr. Kelly grew up as a Jehovah's Witnesses (JW). Since I was not allowed to salute the US flag in my school classroom or elsewhere, imagine my surprise to learn the Jehovah's Witnesses do not allow their members to salute the flag, either. My mother was always particularly critical of the JW religion, stating that their faith was wrong, misguided, and their members would surely go to hell. But I have come to learn that we are alike in many, many ways. Similarities that we share are as follows:

The JWs isolate their children from the world, and forbid them to mingle with non-JWs.

The JWs claim elitism, believing they are the true religion

A JW is not allowed to marry a non-JW.

The JWs do not celebrate birthdays, Halloween, Valentine's Day, Christmas, nor do they celebrate the Fourth of July and other secular holidays.

The Jehovah's Witnesses have many rules, regulations, and obligations designed to keep their members occupied with church issues and evangelism. They are kept so busy that they never have the opportunity to think about the meaning of life, and how they fit into the big picture of the world.

Likewise, the OOM keep their members occupied with numerous farming and food preparation obligations, and are required to use tools and equipment from the past. They labor from sunup 'til sundown, and never have time to think for themselves. An abridged education is also thrown into this mix. Because of my mother's hectic, busy life—and due to her curtailed education—she never learned that JW's had actually given her a gift that eased her life when it came to saluting flags.

The gift mother received was: In 1940, the Jehovah's Witnesses brought a suit before the Supreme Court: *Minersville School District v. Gobitis*. In this suit, JW's argued their children should not be required to stand during the "flag salutation" ceremony, but should be allowed to remain seated.

The Jehovah's Witnesses won this court case.

In 1943, my older siblings and I began attending public school. For the first time ever, we were exposed to the United States flag. In our OOM one-room school house, there was no flag. Therefore, no one worried about saluting the flag, reciting the pledge, and standing at times and remaining seated at other times. All this changed when we attended public school.

My mother knew about flags before we ever set foot in our public schoolroom. "When your classmates stand to salute the flag, you must remain seated," she, firmly, instructed. "Do not participate in saluting the flag in any way."

We remained seated, as our mother had instructed—and our teachers never urged us to stand.

Our mother never knew that Jehovah's Witnesses had earned our right to remain seated. If this had not of happened, our experience in the flag-salutation ceremony could have turned out to be a very dramatic and detrimental experience.

In *Rolling Down Black Stockings*, I tell the story of how I rolled down my black stockings during the flag salutation ceremony. I tried my best to fit in with the other girls in my classroom, who wore socks. But I never actually stood up and saluted the flag.

Inability to salute the flag, the wearing of black stockings, the wearing of plain dresses, of bonnets, were items of separation. We were pilgrims who walked a different path, the path of the past, the path that guaranteed we'd walk alone amongst all others in this world. My classmates walked in the present and wore dresses that represented people of the present world. I simply tried to taste the present at times, and rolled down my black stockings, sneaked into school assemblies, and attended a movie at a local theater,—which were labeled sinful by my religion.

Nonetheless, all this sneaking worked to my advantage when we left the OOM religion. That's how life tricks you at times. You think you're going down the bad road, and it turns out to be the good road.

Because of the shame I felt growing up Old Order Mennonite, once we left the religion, I practiced, "don't tell". In fact, I was still practicing "don't tell" when *Rolling Down Black Stockings* was published in the Spring of 2005. Yet, splashed across the cover were bold "telling" words: *"A memoir of growing up in the Old Order Mennonite Community"*. My memoir forced me to come out—uncomfortable as it was.

A few days after my memoir became available, one of my closest and dearest friends arrived at my front door. She picked up the book, turned it around and over in her hands, and then read the front cover quietly and carefully. With her face awash in astonishment, she said, "Old Order Mennonites! Esther! Aren't these people a little dumb?"

Her word "dumb" floored me. So that's how we appeared to the outside world! But, of course, why not? How could we, the people who walked in the past, appear in any other way?

A sickening feeling wiped across me as I realized it all added up. It wasn't true, of course. We were not born dumb, but made dumb! Made dumb by a religion so that we'd find it difficult to ever leave!

Curtailing our education and making us dress differently would not make us strong. Telling us the outside world was evil and would harm us, telling us that we needed to stay under the religion's protective arms for our safety, made us weak and fearful, and made it unlikely that we would venture outside of our community.

Made to be different so that we couldn't mingle! Made to feel different so that we couldn't speak up for ourselves! Poor pilgrim girls with their special eggs throbbing, throwing off pheromones, capturing pilgrim boys with their special sperm concocted in centuries past. Let these two unite and have the children who will live in pilgrim past.

Having grown up Old Order Mennonite, I know these people aren't dumb. Generally, they are uneasy talking with outsiders, however.

One reason for their uneasiness is their lack of confidence, for they are aware they have been hampered educationally.

A second reason for their uneasiness is due to the huge divide in cultural differences between the people of the past and the people of the present. What would they talk about?

A third reason for their uneasiness stems from fear that is created internally. Because the Old Order Mennonite religion is highly secretive, their people are afraid they'll say something, unintentionally or inadvertently, that they shouldn't. Swift punishments would ensue. Fear numbs the tongue, whether in a secretive religion or in a personal relationship.

Within the confines of their world, Old Order Mennonites are highly intelligent. Ladies excel in cooking and baking, and gentlemen are highly skilled in getting the most corn or wheat out of their acreage. Their quilt-making and furniture-construction will challenge all others in these fields.

Praise amongst humble pilgrims is most rare—to say the least—and great effort is taken to praise the object, not the creator. For instance, a comment on an excellent pie might run like this: "Emma's strawberries make a good pie." Or, rather than receive praise, a prosperous farmer might hear: "With such rich pastureland, it's no wonder your cows swim with milk."

When my good friend made her comment about the Old Order Mennonites being a little dumb, I blurted out some implausible explanation as to why people might see them that way. In truth, the issue of a religion limiting one's education is extremely emotional with me.

Episode 3 of the *Amish in the City* TV series finds Jonas (Amish) diligently studying for his upcoming GED exam. He had received the customary eighth-grade education. Now that he's out in the world, he realizes his education has sorely compromised his ability to compete for jobs.

A City-Dweller actor questions Jonas as to why a religion would limit one's education. Jonas stammers for words, and can't find any possible explanation. He finally admits he doesn't know why, yet doesn't express anger about being denied an education.

It's not surprising that Jonas wouldn't know why his religion limited his education, for he was taught to never question his religion's rules. The natural progression for humans is to see, to question, and to learn. When one is required to accept without questioning, natural flow of learning is impeded.

Jonas doesn't express anger about being denied an education, which surprises some of the City Dwellers. Jonas would have been taught to never show anger. His passivity shows in this episode.

Everyone has heard of the 1973 Roe *v* Wade Supreme Court decision, but how many have heard of the 1972 Wisconsin *v* Yoder ruling? Roe *v* Wade gave women the right to abortion and Wisconsin *v* Yoder gave Amish parents the right to *limit* their children's education. (This right was extended to the OOM and Hutterite parents, as well.)

This 1972 case centered upon protecting the religious rights of parents, and not the rights or needs of children, in education.

The question, naturally, left hanging in the wind is: Why eighth grade? A child is usually twelve or thirteen when in the eighth grade. For most children, puberty begins at this age, give or take a few years. Puberty equals passion, and passion is that stuff which passes from one to another as easily as the flu. Even those raised in most isolated conditions are likely to catch it, no matter how much hand-washing they do.

Limiting their children's education enhances the possibilities that Old Order Mennonite children will stay within the folds of the church's community.

When in my early forties, I decided to further my education. My peers had all attended and graduated from college, and I felt disadvantaged, awkward and timid about joining them in conversation. I enrolled in Danbury College, near Bridgeport, Connecticut, where we lived at the time.

Since I was wary about my adventure, I took what I thought would be a simple course: Interpersonal Communication. Passing this course was easy, for I merely memorized my lessons. In fact, I received an A. In a practical sense, however, I gained nothing from the class. My mind was too blocked with fear for me to open myself up to others.

Eventually, I graduated from the University of Arkansas with honors. I earned a BS in Biology and a minor in Psychology, and was employed by a major pharmaceutical company in Delaware. I worked there for seven years, happily, and then my husband decided he would retire from his job and move to Florida.

We moved to Florida's Gulf side, a little north of Tampa. My husband's dream for his retirement years was to fish and scuba dive. I had little interest in fish or water, but was heavily interested in pen and paper. With close proximity to St. Petersburg University, I enrolled in a creative writing class.

Creative writing enabled me, for the first time, to begin to understand myself. The act of writing with my hand what I was thinking in my brain cleared mind blocks that had been constructed in my childhood. These blocks were built with fear: Don't do this! Don't do that! Watch out! The world will harm you!

Fear was still within me, but writing offered a medium of protection. I could express thoughts on paper, review my words, and examine their comfort and safety. I could erase my thoughts totally, or express them through metaphors, similes, analogies, and other literary figures of speech. Such figures of speech have been utilized in the great stories of *Alice in Wonderland* and the *Wizard of Oz*.

Through these creative writing courses, I began to understand my childhood religion, and what it had meant to me and the members of my family.

In 1954, the year I turned sixteen, mother was overjoyed about my birthday. It had nothing to do with my birthday, however, but everything to do with the fact I could finally obtain my driver's license. With my license, I could drive my brother Mark to Youngstown Receiving Hospital on Saturday morning, where he was scheduled to receive shock treatments for depression.

Previously, my sister Ruth had driven Mark to Youngstown for these treatments. However, the nursing home where she now worked, had requested that she shift her schedule, making her unavailable on Saturdays.

Mark worked the five weekdays at the Columbiana Pump Company, which made treatments on Saturday necessary. Equally important was that he had Sunday off, for he needed that day for recuperation before returning to his weekly job.

By this time, Mark had earned enough money to purchase a gem of a car: a slick, new red 1954 Ford. Quite protective of his jewel, Mark cautioned his younger siblings about playing around his car. If we forgot, he emitted the growl of an angry tiger, frightening his younger siblings, scattering us every which way.

As with all cars in that day, his Ford had manual transmission, which meant one had to coordinate between a clutch and gear shift in one second of time, which greatly complicated a "new learner's" ease of use.

On Saturday morning Mark would drive his new Ford to Youngstown while I rode in the passenger seat. On the return trip, I drove while Mark lay in the back seat.

Upon arrival at the hospital, the nurses greeted Mark, and then took him down a long hallway into a back room. I sat in the waiting room, where several hours passed before I'd see Mark again. When the nurses returned with him, Mark was extremely pale and disoriented, and with legs wobbly and unsteady. Two nurses, one on each side, ushered him into the room and waited with him until I brought his Ford around. The nurses then assisted Mark to the car and put him in the back seat. There, he sprawled across its distance, curling and folding as necessary to fit his six-foot body into the four-foot seat. The nurses returned into the hospital and it was up to me to drive Mark safely home.

As usual, I had paid little attention as Mark had driven to the hospital. I hadn't even noticed that Youngstown was full of hills. Now driving, I learned that not only did Youngstown have hills, Youngstown had mountains. Or, so it seemed. And placed at the very top of each mountain was a stoplight. My nerves bubbled within my stomach as I approached each apex, for coordinating shift, brake, clutch, and gas pedal was not easy for me. I no longer worried about getting a scratch on his car, but worried about a crushed bumper due to back drifting.

As I feared, with each stop on a hill, Mark's beautiful new Ford coasted backward—a few inches seeming like feet—sometimes yards. Fortunately, drivers behind me stopped ample distances away, for some reason. My tenseness didn't leave me until I returned to familiar country roads once again. There, nothing impeded my way except a stray cow or a farmer sitting atop his horse-drawn hay wagon.

Mark knew none of this, for he was seemingly asleep in the back seat. I heard groaning at times, and thought he might vomit, but he never did. Once home, Mom assisted him as he climbed the stairs and went into his bedroom. He stayed there for the duration of the weekend. Then, on Monday, he arose and returned to his job at the Pump Company in Columbiana.

The shock treatments helped Mark's depression, and he was able to stop them—at least for a few years. When twenty-one, Mark signed up to fulfill his Conscience Objector's draft duties. He served as an orderly who worked in the stockroom at Cleveland hospital, and was there when we moved to Akron. After two years, he fulfilled his required duty time. But, by that time Mark's depression had returned. He checked himself into a receiving hospital in Cleveland, where he received treatment.

During our early Akron years, Mark's depression continued to plague and haunt him. Relationships and marriages happened and un-happened. I am happy to report that Mark, now nearly eighty, enjoys good health and is in good spirit. He attributes his good health to his heavy vitamin and mineral regimen, which he has studied extensively and promotes with gusto to everyone he encounters. His knowledge, which he readily voices, has earned him the nickname, Dr. Mark.

Dr. Mark's health also comes from regular frequent exercises at the gym. His good spirits come from his relationship with Pat and his high involvement in the lives of his grandchildren. His high intellect is nourished through extensive reading, which consists of two newspapers a day, scholarly magazines such as *Scientific American Journal* and *Consumer Reports*, and just about everything he can get his hands on.

Mark earned his GED when he retired at sixty-five.

My sisters Grace, Ruth, and Sarah, when in their teens, had to quit school early because of the OOM rule. Grace and Ruth, also, obtained their GED's later in life: Grace after working for a hospital kitchen; Ruth after working years in a dental office.

Sarah progressed from working for a laundry in downtown Akron to sterilizing surgical equipment for a hospital in Cuyahoga Falls. Before she had a chance to retire and earn her GED, she died when she was fifty years old.

A few years prior to her death, Sarah had suffered a severe head injury received in an automobile accident. Shortly, thereafter, she was diagnosed with early onset Alzheimer's Disease, and lived for a few years in a nursing home. Upon her death, an autopsy, conducted by the University Hospital in Cleveland, confirmed her Alzheimer's diagnosis.

KNOWLEDGE

Is like walking on rock-solid ground.

SECRECY

Is like skating on thin, slippery ice.

CHAPTER 6

The Secretive Pilgrim

Time moved unbearably slow before our move to Akron. Life amounted to work, work, and more work. Get up in the morning . . . feed the chickens . . . cook the breakfast . . . weed the garden . . . make the supper . . . wash the dishes . . . go to bed you sleepy head. My only escape was at school. All this changed when we moved.

It was as if I had stepped into a swift-moving boat that took me from past to present—a boat I had to quickly board, or drown. No other alternatives existed. Then, before any bell sounded or any clock chimed, I was living there.

Upon disembarking, a most exhilarating and intoxicating feeling of freedom washed over me, a feeling a butterfly must experience when first stepping out of a chrysalis. Somehow I knew that all my straps of bondage had loosened, and I was free to live up to my potential, whatever that might be.

Church was a major part of our life before we moved to Akron, and church became a major part of our life afterward. The difference was in the way the two churches conducted their services. Our former church operated in past time; our chosen new church operated in present time.

The church of the past had tightly-strung, stoic Old Order Mennonites who sat like boards in pews, and who suppressed even a slightest urge to sneeze. The church of the present had Full Gospel worshippers who shouted and stomped the floors and swayed their hips as they worshipped God.

Sermons in the Old Order church were delivered with barely a fluctuation in decibel level. It was easy to come away without feeling emotionally or intellectually moved.

Sermons in the Full Gospel church boomed from the preacher's mouth. "You must be born again!" he shouted, making the floors shake and rafters quake, and audiences aching with emotion. Shouts of "Amen!" filled the air, followed by rhythmic clapping of hands, swaying of hips, and grinning to the person on your left and to the person on your right.

Next came a lip-smack to person on your right, and a "May God be with you!" to the person on your left. Lip smacks became hip smacks: a hip smack to the person on your left, a hip smack to the person on your right, setting off chain reactions that encompassed everyone in your row. A hip-smacking, hugging train soon formed, and quickly became a chug-chug chugging train that moved into the aisle. Chug-chugs went to the front, chug-chugs went to the back, then chug-chugs circled the room three times. Not content to stop there, chug-chugs moved out the door . . . with a wave-wave to all as they exited the room. Hey! Hey! Isn't this fun!

Turn around . . . touch the ground . . . tie your shoe . . . skip to my loo . . . pick up sticks . . . robot in . . . robot out.

Confession of transgression was easily accomplished in the Full Gospel church. Go to the altar . . . tell God you are sorry . . . put in some money . . . you'll be forgiven . . . get on the people train . . . go to the restaurant . . . turn around . . . touch the ground . . . tie your shoe . . . skip to my loo.

Confession was not easily accomplished when we were with the Old Order Mennonites, however. There, you'd be called before the member congregation where you'd have to confess before all. It amounted to self-flagellation with a great deal of pain, and acknowledgment of the fact that you were bad, because they said you were bad. Since God would forgive you, they would as well.

On the fifteen of October in1953, a few weeks after our father had turned fifty, he died from pneumonia, a complication of being bedfast for seven years. During those long and difficult years, mother patiently cared for my father at home. She recruited her children to feed Father and to help turn his sheet-wrapped bony body from side to side. In situations involving intimate care, such as in use of bedpans and in giving baths, we were not allowed to help.

At forty-seven, Mother entered widowhood in a haggard condition. Not only was she tired, but she was lost. All her life, she had been taught that man is above the woman, and that it is a woman's duty to take care of the house and the children, and the man's duty to take care of all financial affairs.

OOM children turned all their earned money over to their parents until twenty-one. Most females were married before that age, and her husband then managed the money. A woman unfortunate enough to be widowed would enter into this state clueless about money situations. Generally, the oldest son would step in and manage financial affairs for the family.

My father's illness confined him to bed, which put him in a submissive situation. My mother could have taken a dominant role at any time, for what could father have managed? Dominance was foreign to her, however, and guilt feelings kept her subjugated and subservient. Therefore, she consulted Papa in situations of finances and solicited his opinions on how best to manage the household. But the time came when Papa's thinking was no longer rational. At such times, she'd run out of Papa's bedroom and shake her fists into the air. "Sick minds make sick decisions, children! Don't ever forget that!"

When my father died, the community consoled mother with comments such as, "You're young, yet. You'll find another man."

Mother angrily retorted, "I don't want another man! At my age, all another man would want me for is to cook and clean for him. I'm done with all that!"

My mother's answer reflected how far she had grown in personal independence. She didn't need love, for that only meant she'd have to serve another again, to be under another's control. She was tired of that position and wanted to drive her own train.

Love did come to mother in a round-about way. It began in her mailbox. Crouching in the midst of letters was a packet of information from Spears Clinic in Denver, Colorado. The packet contained literature regarding an alternative-medicine therapy. I don't know if mother had solicited this information, or if someone had ordered it for her, but alternative "something" was the very thing she needed about then.

Immediately, upon opening and reading the literature packet, we noticed that she lifted her feet higher when walking from chore to chore. She carried the packet in the bib of her apron when she peeled potatoes for supper, and did other cooking chores. It was there when she moved from cooking to cleaning, and from cleaning to sewing. Frequently, as she worked, she pulled the packet from its bib hide-away and showed the literature to her children. She explained alternative medicine to us, but we couldn't grasp the concept. And we couldn't understand her need for something that seemed such a departure from our normal way of doing things.

My mother was not dissuaded. The idea that one could find health merely by changing one's diet left her breathless. *Innovative*, the literature claimed, which she repeated to us over and over again. "It's innovative! You can turn your health around in one week. All you need do is to go to their clinic for intensive therapy." She then inhaled deeply and said once again, "One week and I can be well!"

She didn't seem to worry that the clinic was located in Denver, Colorado, which was west of the Mississippi River. Mother had never been farther west than Indiana.

"You'll have to fly," we told her.

"I have to regain my health," she replied.

"You'll be leaving your children alone," neighbors told her.

"I need to regain my health!" she replied.

And, surprisingly, mother didn't need to worry about money, either. It seems that father had a sizeable amount of inheritance in his bank account, (money he had received when his father died), money that now became mother's money. As long as Father was alive, mother had been forbidden to touch it.

Eight fearful children drove their mother to the Youngstown, Ohio, airport and put their frail mother on a plane. We had no clear idea of where Denver was; we just knew it was in Colorado. Colorado seemed far away; Colorado had mountains. "Denver is a mile high," our mother had said, as if this would make us feel better. But it didn't. All seemed foreign.

And we had no idea of what alternative therapy was either, no matter how much our mother tried to explain it to us. We worried we might never see her again, not alive, that is.

Soon our fears were put aside when we received letters from our mother. *The clinic says I need to wash all the poisons out of my body first. Then they'll put me on a healthy diet. So, for now, all I'm allowed is grape juice. I've had only grape juice for one week. I've lost a lot of weight. I feel better already.*

We shook our heads and wished our mother would come home.

Subsequent letters touted the benefits of alternative therapy, and how much it had already helped her. Indeed, Mother seemed to be regaining her health. Then, suddenly, her letters were different, as she reported on her latest new alternative therapy. She had found a new religion, one that sumed every sentence in her letters. She called the religion Full Gospel, and reported that believers spoke in tongues and were healed through prayer.

Full gospel, in expression, was just about as opposite of a religion as you could get from the stoic and passive OOMs. Yet, her letters crowed about her newly-found religion, and how her friend, a lady she had met at the clinic, had introduced her to the Oral Roberts' radio programs. *When I get home*, she wrote, *we'll buy a radio so you children can hear him for yourselves.*

After three months of alternative therapy in Denver, our mother returned home, her face blooming with her new love. And true to her promise, she purchased a radio. It was our first radio ever, and extremely appealing to teenaged children. Wisely, she cautioned, "We can use our radio for God or we can use our radio for the devil. It's all in how you turn the dial. In our house we shall use our radio for God."

When our mother went to town, we found a new way of life as well. We discovered *freedom* could be ours with the turn of a dial. Independence made us stronger. But still we were obedient in a sneaky way. When our mother was home we listened to what she played on the radio. When she was out shopping, or picking green beans in the garden, or visiting her sisters, we tuned in radio stations that played country music. We kicked up our feet and sang along with radio songs, carefully, returning the dial to where our mother had left it, back to where she received her religious programs. Our "Mama cat" never knew that her "children-mice" played while she was away.

During one of Oral Roberts' radio programs, mother learned about Rex Humbard. To her delight, Rev. Humbard practiced Full Gospel religion, also. And, best of all, he conducted tent revival meetings practically in our back yard.

The charismatic Reverend Rex may have been new to mother, but he was not new to the world of evangelism. He had preached mostly in Texas and in other southern states. Only recently had he set up a tent revival ministry in the Akron, Ohio, area. Because she could not drive, mother enlisted her children, the ones old enough to have obtained a license, to take her from our Columbiana home to his meetings.

Emotional meetings stirred within mother, and she couldn't get enough Full Gospel. When Reverend Rex announced that he intended to stay in Akron, and asked members of his audience to join him in his ministry, mother stood up and promised to help.

In the summer of 1955, less than two years after my father's death, mother announced to the church, to our relatives, neighbors, and friends that our little Germantown Road bungalow was for sale. She would be moving to Akron, Ohio. Not only would she be moving, but all of her eight children, now between the ages of twelve and twenty-two, would be moving as well.

Community members were astonished. "Why make this drastic change?" they asked.

Adamantly, Mother proclaimed, "I've found the true religion! I can't live on man-made religion anymore. I'm hungry for the Word of God!"

Community members scratched their heads as they pondered her statements. *Can't live on man-made religion! Desires the Word of God!* Her shocking statements were like slaps in their faces.

"We are the true religion!" one said.

Another said, "You've been taken in by a false prophet!"

Their warning statements did no good. Mother was adamant in her belief that Old Order Mennonite rules and regulations did not come from the Bible, but were man-made. She assigned wearing thick, black, heavy stockings to man-made ideas. Coverings, capes, peasant dresses, and unfashionable black-laced shoes went into the "man-made-ideas" group as well. She even assigned the pitiful and painful curtailing of education, that had hobbled her for life, as a man-made rule.

She would move to Akron where she could attend a church that preached messages aligned to her new way of thinking; a church that focused on healing the sick and saving the souls of the wicked; a church where women were as welcomed as men to give testimony for what God had done for them.

Since OOMs practiced an emotionless religion, the community did not understand mother. They had heard rumors about the fervor that being "born again" created within some people. To them, such people simply wore out the seat of their pants and the soles of their shoes in their emotional worship of God. Old Order Mennonites believed worship of God should be done with simplicity and reverence, and with a humble spirit.

When the community heard of our mother's decision to move to Akron, they gossiped amongst themselves. "Has she gone bananas?" they asked one another, and then agreed, "We have to stop her!" Groups of two, often four, sometimes more, visited our mother in our little Germantown Road house. They tried to persuade our mother to change her mind. All their talking made no difference. "I desire the Word of God!" said mother.

"Then, please, think of your children!" they begged. "At least, think of them!"

My mother replied, "I am thinking of them! That's why I'm moving."

They shook their heads as they walked from our house, mumbling, and repeating: "Think of your children. At least, think of your children."

Our Germantown Road House didn't sell, undoubtedly due to our mother's disobedience, but that didn't deter her from moving to Akron. She purchased the house in Akron with inheritance money our father had received, which was now rightfully hers.

Upon arrival in Akron, mother threw herself wholeheartedly into Bible study and prayer groups. She attended all the frequent services Rev. Humbard scheduled for his church members. Through religion, she integrated herself into her new world.

My siblings and I were reluctant to throw ourselves into such an emotional religion. Yet, we needed friends; we sorely needed friends. Before our move to Akron, a few of my older siblings had been on dates, but none had experienced a serious love relationship. When we arrived in Akron, most of us were into our heady, ripe-and-ready age. Rev. Humbard offered a program for teens in our condition. He called it his Full Gospel Youth Service, which took place every Sunday evening.

The Youth Service began with the singing of hymns and other Christian songs. Most of the songs were familiar to us, and we readily joined in. Hymn singing progressed into holding of hands, then hugging the person next to you. The Reverend then asked young people who had already accepted God, to come forward and offer personal testimonies. He followed with a charismatic talk about the need to be saved, and the need to be born again. He pleaded with all the young people to come forward and accept God.

At first, my siblings and I dug in our heels. We were humble people who prayed in the closet, after all. We didn't even say a spoken grace. Showy displays embarrassed us. Statements such as one needed to be born again to go to heaven seemed farfetched. Our mother may have been swept totally off her feet, but we weren't going to make rash decisions.

But then came . . . the hug from the person on our left . . . a warm hand grasping our hand from the right . . . at a time when we needed friends . . . we sorely needed friends . . . so tired of walking alone . . . of being alone . . . of not being up to snuff with our stuff. Resistance no longer seemed important.

I entered school as a junior in Akron's North High school; my younger brothers attending Jennings Jr. High. As I had in Columbiana, I concentrated on getting good grades. Getting good grades made me feel valued.

Mother spent most hours of each day studying to be an Evangelist, and allowed her children to fend, according to their maturity and ability. After all, she didn't know much about how young people should act in the world. And, after all, we had fended for ourselves all those years our father was sick. And we had fended for ourselves all those months she had spent in Denver recuperating with alternative treatments. We felt relief that she now wanted to occupy herself studying to be an Evangelist.

Mother basically turned her children over to God, and asked Him to keep us on the straight and narrow. We could hear her praying for us when we returned home from our dates. At this point in her life, Mother only insisted that we attend church, which we readily obeyed, for that's where we found our dates.

Meanwhile, Mother noticed she lacked the proper social graces society required of an Evangelist. Although unable to label them as such, her manners and actions were that of a peasant farmwife. When she looked at her daughters, she saw they needed refinement, as well. She determined that a makeover was in order.

She learned that a Charm School operated in Polsky's Department Store in downtown Akron, the equivalent to Macy's today, and enrolled in the class. "Only one person in our family need take these costly lessons," she said to her daughters, "so I'll take the class and pass along all I learn."

Indeed, Charm School was exactly what she (we) needed. We learned proper use of make-up, the appropriate way to walk, to stand, the essentials of cultivated speech, the manners needed to interact with a diverse group of people, those whom we had formerly labeled as strangers.

We soon realized we were as green as the vegetables we grew in our garden.

Let me diverse here and say that part of the healing process when breaking through mind blocks is *humor*. If you can look back on your former self and laugh, you're in good recovery. With this in mind, I have categorized our Charm School lessons into two groups. The first group is labeled "Peasant Girl" (the OOM girl) and the second group is labeled "Modern Girl" (the Akron girl). Since I have some of Mom's actual notebooks written during her Charm School classes, I have used italics when quoting her notes.

Taking a bath

Peasant Girl:

OOM women and teenage girls do not shave under their arms or legs. Neither do they cut their hair.

Baths are taken once a week—on Saturday night.

Modern Girl:

Take a bath every morning. A lady needs to shave under her arms and her legs twice a week.

Social graces

Peasant Girl:

As you might expect, OOM women do not have time to bother with social graces. If you asked one of them the best way to approach a chair, she would exclaim: "Who has time to sit on a chair?"

After a full day of caring for children, grandchildren, cooking, canning, and sewing for her big family, who could blame her for not bothering with social graces? But, if you pressed further, she would say, "The best way to sit on a chair is to plop into it."

Modern Girl:

How to sit on a chair: In walking up to the left side of a chair, stand directly in front of the chair with a left hesitation; when walking up from the right side, stand in a right hesitation. The back leg should always touch the chair so we do not need to look back to see where the chair is, and we had a good look at it when we walked up to the chair.

Now, sit on the chair, not all the way back. Place the right hand, palm down, on the front corner of the chair and slip all the way back in the chair. At the same time you are slipping back, place the right foot over the left one, crossing at the ankles, keeping both flat on the floor, at an angle to the right corner of the chair. The soles of the shoes should never be seen.

Accessories

Peasant Girl:

OOM women would consider accessories vain and a nuisance. Babies would play with a dangling necklace; an earring could fall into the soup; a bracelet might get caught in the meat grinder; a ring on a finger could fall into the milk bucket.

Modern Girl:

My mother writes about hat veils, when and where to wear a veil. She devotes an entire section to white gloves—when a proper lady wears them.

Other pages tell about jewelry, when to wear it, and how to clean different pieces. Others discuss the use of scarves, belts, collars and cuffs.

Greetings:

Peasant Girl:

OOM women don't bother much with proper social graces. Their handshakes are warm and friendly, and their greetings are always the same.

"How-do-you-do!" an OOM woman will say upon meeting someone for the first time. She'll quickly follow with, "And, who are you?" It's very important that her visitor have a proper OOM name before she'll go any further.

Should the stranger say, "I'm David Yoder's boy!" she'll say, "I'll be! I should have known. You sure look like your Papa. Well, come on in."

If the stranger gives her a surname she doesn't know, she'll say, "I have two bushels of apples to put up before dark. Don't mean to be rude." The conversation will end with her turn of heel and her closing of the door.

Modern Girl:

Examples of good etiquette are:

> *I would like you to know . . .*
> *Do you know . . .*
> *I want you to meet . . .*

The proper rules for introducing people, according to rank, are:

> *Always introduce ladies first, except when it's one of the royal family, president or clergy man.*

Another rule says:

> *A lady can choose to shake hands, but must always offer her hand when she is hostess. The "pump handle" fashion is incorrect.*

*   *   *

With Bible study and "body" study completed, mother had one more hurdle to conquer before she could become an Evangelist for God. After all, God had called her, and she had heard His voice most clearly. Obedience to God had always been of utmost importance to her.

Learning proper social graces had been easy for mother to accomplish, but learning to speak with ease in front of people was an absolute terror for her. Nevertheless, with her usual unswerving determination, she learned all she could about public speaking. She then practiced and practiced.

But speaking seemed confrontational to her, something she had learned early on that she should not be. Fear flooded her every cell.

Other messages, as well, assaulted her brain: Men should fill places of leadership within a church; women are to be quiet and take places of submission; a woman's place is in the home; if a woman wants to talk to God, let her go into her closet and pray quietly.

Mother was adamant about her call, however, which she had received directly from God. And, as far as she was concerned, her God was sexless. She would praise and serve Him, and she would label the numerous OOM sexist rules as man-made ideas.

With a passion comparable to St. Peter and St. Paul, mother loved God. In spite of her fears, she would tell the world what He had done for her. She wanted to testify, should have been able to testify, yet when she tried, "fear demons" grabbed her tongue. She wrestled with her demons, and then wrapped them all up into one giant super ball. Wound tightly in passion, she nervously awaited her moment to bounce.

Her time came. After Reverend Rex's sermon, he asked members to stand and testify about what God had done for them.

Mother shot out of her seat and was the first on her feet. She delivered her testimony in one long memorized swoop, and then collapsed back into her seat, as graciously as she could.

Reverend Rex's congregations were huge, and those witnessing mother's testimony to God were many. At first the congregation was deathly quiet, as if digesting what had taken place. Then one person stood and clapped for mother. Others followed, and more and more, until the entire congregation stood and clapped for what they had heard. My mother was pleased that she had touched so many.

How proud I was of mother on that day! Upon leaving the Old Order Mennonite religion, mother had many challenges to face, and her greatest challenge was in taking a role that would place her in a prominent position, a confrontational place of sorts. We were to remain in the background as passive people, people who never spoke in front of groups.

Such a position would have been hard for an OOM man to acquire, also—for both men and women practiced a religion that demanded non-confrontation and extreme humility, the sort of religion that made passive people.

*   *   *

When seventeen, I arrived in Akron. In actuality, I arrived from the past into present time.

Although, scholastically, I did well in my new school, I was immature socially and culturally. Dr. Erik Erickson, in his Eight Stages of Life, predicted one could pass through physical stages and yet, socially, remain as a child.

Now that I was able to dress like my classmates and have my hair cut, I could finally be like them. In most ways this was true, but one huge difference stood like a rock between us. Actually, it was just one year that was as big as a rock, and it had to do with the fact that I had failed. I now was a year older than my classmates, which made me different—once again.

As everyone knows, when you're in high school, age is very important. You never know when someone will ask, "How old are you?" Or, you never know when you'll be celebrating a classmate's sixteenth birthday and someone will suddenly ask, "When will you be sixteen?" These are natural questions for teens.

The fact that I was older made me feel "less than"—and an explanation would not be easy. Could I say I flunked because of Old Order Mennonite restrictions, and go into all that pain without falling apart? It was simpler to tell a lie and to make myself a year younger.

Lying, like secrets, never strengthens a person, but adds stress to one's life. Lying requires vigilance, for one misspoken word or sentence could reveal your deception. Lying is like quicksand under your feet.

In my case, lying had drained away much energy over the years, energy that could have been better used in productive ways.

Childhood cultural experiences differed greatly between my new peers and me. They had grown up attending movies, learning to dance, listening to radio music, appreciating art, reading fiction, and experiencing entertainment activities that had been forbidden to me. Conversation became difficult. How could I converse about the hours I spent pulling weeds, about cold mornings milking cows, about Saturday afternoons churning butter, about summer days spent canning peaches and peas (not in the same jar), about the Monday mornings I had spent hanging wash for a family of ten on the clothesline?

*   *   *

Before moving to Akron, I had never owned nor worn a bathing suit. Frankly, I wasn't allowed to swim. In the first place, OOM girls weren't allowed to bare their bodies, other than their head and feet. In the second place, OOM girls weren't allowed to get "dirty" pond water into their "place" where the sun didn't shine.

All was different for my brothers, however, who frequented secluded swimming holes that appeared in our pastures. With little care, they disrobed, tossed their clothes aimlessly aside, and jumped in. OOM boys just never had to worry about dirty pond water getting into private places—simply because they weren't entrusted with beautiful and precious eggs.

In my first year of arrival in Akron, I wanted to swim with my new peers. I began taking swimming lessons at the YWCA. After months of lessons, I could barely manage to float. But my float emboldened me to the point that I agreed to join my newly discovered best girlfriend, Alice, on vacation. We planned to go to her uncle's cabin in Michigan. If she had mentioned that her uncle owned a motor boat, and that we'd spend the weekend water skiing, I missed it.

A motorboat purring down a river is quite mesmerizing. While Alice drove the boat, her uncle showed me how to water ski. How hard could that be? I asked myself.

Alice then took her turn. Skiing still looked easy. *If I can float, I can do it*, I deluded myself.

Bravely, I took the towrope, but then waves of doubt hardened my leg and arm muscles.

"Come on up," said Uncle, revving the motor. As soon as the boat shot through the water, I was literally in over my head. I ended up in the water and had to be rescued by Uncle.

I should have confessed from the beginning that I didn't know how to swim well enough to water ski, but I wanted to fit in.

As I write this, I am grateful that I watched the *Amish in the City* series a few years ago. I generally can redeem my actions by equating my experiences with someone's from the show. In this case, it was Mose, the main Amish actor, who placed himself in a most dangerous swimming situation, even though he knew how to swim.

Mose swam into the wide Pacific Ocean and swam out too far. Fortunately, he was being televised for the *Amish in the City* reality show and was quickly rescued.

We both were rescued, but the fact remains that when we journey from the past into the present, we venture into situations far beyond our capability. Part of this is due to our need for acceptance, and part of this is due to our newness in making choices for ourselves. Far too often, we end up just going along with the crowd.

*   *   *

Before moving to Akron I had never danced. I had watched the smooth moves of my peers on North High's dance floor, and they appeared to be so relaxed. But when a boy asked me to dance, I was as stiff as a stick.

I tried to mirror the actions of my peers, who glided as if on skates across the floor. "Unchained Melody" was a favorite in that day, a song that should have unchained any stick. Yet, I remained inflexible.

Enough of these agonies: I decided to learn to dance! Through conversation in school I had learned that an Italian club in downtown Akron held dances on Saturday evenings. "Everyone's welcomed," the rumor mill said. I decided to try it in secret, for I didn't want my peers to know I was dance deprived.

Since I had grown up virtually on another planet, I had no idea that boys came to the club to pick up dates.

My first night went like this: After a few rounds of dancing, a partner would suggest that we go for a hamburger. "My car's right here," he would say. "We can go to Sam's Place. It's right down the street, can't be farther than a mile or two."

After enjoying our hamburger and a milkshake, my "dancing partner" did not take me back to the club. Instead, he stopped along some dark, unfamiliar road for smooching. Quick thinking made me say: "Sorry, I'm having my period," which I had learned from after-church service experiences was such a turn-off for men.

"How about next Saturday evening?" he then asked.

"Okay." I quickly responded, agreeing to anything that would get me quickly returned to the club.

On the following week, I didn't go for hamburgers with him. Instead, I offered another excuse: "Sorry, I have to get my car home. My brother needs it for work."

Predictably, by the third week I had run out of plausible excuses. And, predictably, I couldn't be forthright, honest, and candidly say, *sorry, I came here to learn to dance. I don't want to go for hamburgers.* Instead, I went into my familiar passive mode and quit my dance lessons.

Inability to be forthright, honest and candid leads to "beating around the bush"—a well-known axiom. People who beat around the bush end up destroying bushes, but nothing more is accomplished. Trust has to be earned before truth will be forthcoming. Survival of the individual is, and always will be, the primary motivator of one's behavior.

Some might argue that one always has the choice to be honest. One can choose honesty over survival. Is this not where true martyrdom enters the picture? True martyrs choose honesty over survival. Did I need to be a martyr in these situations? I think not.

*   *   *

In my early years in the City, dating presented a problem for me. How does one act on a date? I began to watch my classmates for a "monkey see, monkey do" lesson. They held each other's hands, whispered sweet nothings in each other's ears, stared into each other's eyes, as if each was the only person in this world. I longed for such individuality, for believing I was special.

Since Old Order Mennonites never expressed their love in public, and parents never expressed their love in words or actions in front of their children, I had no idea of how dating progressed. I thought I knew how dating initiated, however. It went something like this: A boy approached a girl, (the opposite was inappropriate); he expressed an interest in the girl (hopefully, me). I must be elusive and passive. I must not voice any choice, but instead allow the boy to believe he was the master.

Loving interaction between a man and a woman was secretive in my OOM community. Although I had never seen my parents kiss, hug, hold hands, say loving words to one another, or even look at one another tenderly, I surmised that they did. I saw the results of their love in sixteen little hand-and-foot prints that filled every inch of our Columbiana bungalow.

In my early teen years, I had read a small amount of literature on the subject of dating, sneakily, of course, which necessitated gleaning tidbits here and there. All this left me clueless when I first started dating.

My first boyfriend soon left me for another girl. Not knowing what I had done wrong, I blamed my dating failure on my plumpness. I dieted, slimmed down, and that turned men's heads. Turning heads, when a pilgrim, is as addictive as valium. From then on, I focused only on attention-seeking behaviors.

My behaviors were validated when, years later, I watched Ruth and Naomi on the *Amish in the City* reality show. The television series portrays the two girls discarding their Amish dress and donning most skimpy bikinis shortly upon their arrival at their Los Angeles mansion, their home for the duration of the series.

With bodies bearing no more than the fig leaves of Eve, the two girls paraded into the swimming pool area. The flattering comments offered by the City Dwellers' would have swollen any pilgrim girl's head.

Going from attention-starved to attention-gorged happened soon after my graduation from Akron's North High School in 1957. I was hired as a secretary by the B.F.Goodrich Co.—a major tire manufacturer in that day. There, I met the man that I would marry within a year. We recently celebrated our fiftieth anniversary.

My husband and I are very different people. He, the perfectionist, operates within his left brain. I, the artist, operate within my right brain. By blending our brains, we become a whole.

More likely, I can attribute our fifty years of marriage to mother's words of wisdom. In my youngest teenage years, I had asked how someone managed to get married. She said, "You have to be a good cook. The best way to a man's heart is through his stomach." I dismissed her words at the time, believing such talk was Old Order Mennonite chatter. To my amazement, she turned out to be right—in an odd sort of way.

In my childhood, children were spanked, a rather confrontational punishment, if you ask me. As children matured, shunning, a non-confrontational punishment, replaced spanking. Shunning was definitely the choice of punishment for adults. Women did not have enough power to shun, but would engage in shunning when ordered by her husband or any other male in the family or church.

An Old Order Mennonite man will shun his wife to keep her in line. I've never seen any punishment used by a wife to keep her husband in line. I suspect a wife has her ways, but all would have to been done in secret.

It's most important that the OOM woman be humble, yet OOM women are some of the best cooks you can imagine. I once made the mistake of praising an OOM lady for the wonderful lunch she had prepared, for, indeed, it was delicious. The lady bowed her head, and then glanced up at her husband, who sat at the table's end. Her husband shook his head back and forth, indicating that she could not accept my praise. Our poor hostess sat with bowed head and couldn't say another word. Everyone at the table felt her hurt and stopped eating, except her husband. Honestly, I don't know what he experienced; I only know he continued dishing food into his mouth.

Shunning is used by the Old Order Mennonite men as a way of controlling their women. And shunning is used by the church, as well, an institution controlled by males, to keep members in line. Some definitions for shunning are: avoiding, rejecting, shrinking from, and ignoring. Shunning, highly antisocial, is meant to make someone feel unloved, undesired, and alone. When living within a closed communal society, where you are already cut off from the outside world, shunning is particularly hurtful.

The hurt generated within the Old Order Mennonite community due to shunning is most obvious in the squabbling that goes on amongst members. Squabbling can quickly lead to schisms, where one group breaks away and forms an offshoot community.

Shunning is about control and power and has nothing to do with love. A husband shuns his wife because, according to his religion, God placed man above the woman, which made him believe he had the right, and even the duty, to control his woman for perceived or actual wrongdoings.

In my growing-up days, the women had to just "put up" with shunning. A woman with ten children and no money certainly had no options. Non-surprisingly, it was the women in my childhood community who visited doctors and asked for nerve pills or nerve tonic.

*   *   *

A pilgrim child grows up in a garden of secrets. And secrets can put you on the slipperiest of slopes. Secrets overheard—and not intended for your ears—can put you on a sled riding over black ice.

I had not intended to be sneaky on that morning, had not intended that at all. But, being in the adjacent room, words drifted my way, drifted into my ears—words that would awaken any young girl's ears.

"I think that's why she can't have babies," said my aunt.

"You don't say!" responded my mother, and further conversation ensued.

Since these words were said in secret, I had no way of asking: "Mother, what does that mean? Why can't she have babies?"

It was in the early1960's when I found myself in "need". My husband and I had planned for a better life, one better than either of us had experienced as children. We had a young son, and wanted more, but not yet, not now, not until we prepared a firm foundation for our future. To accomplish this, we both worked for Goodrich, and my husband studied for an engineering degree in the evening.

Information about upcoming birth control pills was at a feverish pitch on airwaves and in newspapers. "It will change the life of women!" said voices that clamored in offices, in coffees and teas, at parties, and wherever people gathered. "Women, for once, can determine when they want a baby. Couples can finally control the size of their family."

Unfortunately, such help was promised on the morrow—and I needed help on the day.

But I had help. I had a photographic memory that bloomed like a flower within me, which provided me with the very help I now sought. Surprisingly, and strengthening, this memory gave me peace and power. I could control my destiny. My husband and I could achieve our dream, after all.

Sharing my situation with my husband made me uneasy. He was busy, I rationalized, studying as he did for his degree, working part-time, serving in the Army Reserve. Why concern him with my late-period problem? Hadn't the women in my childhood community handled such matters on their own? They did, according to my memory, which I replayed in my head.

♥

It's morning. I'm at the kitchen sink in my childhood home. I'm washing dishes. A mere six feet from me are my mother and aunt. They are peeling apples for canning, and they are conversing while they do so. They drop the apple peels into the slop bucket as they work; peels that will later be fed to squealing pigs.

As usual, my mother and aunt talk about customary community happenings: such things as who wore what? And, was it plain enough? About Uncle Joe's stroke . . . etc . . . etc . . . . about food . . . a new recipe . . . that mouth-watering cherry-topped chocolate cake that they planned to bake for Sunday dinner. All was usual stuff that comprised their conversation while I was in the kitchen.

After drying my last dish I went into the adjacent dining room, tarrying a few minutes as I looked out the back window. A fresh array of blooms had appeared on the petunias and pansies. Their vivid colors intoxicated me, and soon I was lost in their beauty. Suddenly, I heard non-typical words being spoken in the kitchen, words that grabbed my attention.

"You know why she can't get pregnant, don't you?" my aunt asked.

"No," mother answered, "I know she wants a baby in the worse way. Why can't she get pregnant?"

"It's because, when first married, she didn't want children so soon. So she used turpentine to make her period come. I think she did it too often. Now, when she wants babies, she can't have them."

♥

How strange for me to overhear this conversation for, in my childhood home, talks regarding periods, how babies were conceived, born, or anything with the slightest sexual connotation was treated like CIA-classified information. Assuredly, mother did not know I was in the next room, and close enough to overhear.

Today I marvel that Old Order Mennonite women, known for absolute subservience, sneakily controlled their family size. Darwin's evolution meant survival of the fittest, and the fittest does not always look the strongest, or the most muscled. Fittest often means the wittiest, the cleverest—and MOST OFTEN means those who have the greatest need.

Words spoken in secret, and overheard by another, are like fertile seeds in the soil. You may even forget such words exist, but with a little sun, a little rain, a **big need**, seeds anchor and quickly sprout into fully-blossomed flowers. Remembering the secret that bloomed within me gave me comfort—for now I had a tool—and my tool had a name. Its name was turpentine.

I planned to take my "tool" on a weekend when my husband was out of town, on his once-a-month Army Reserve training. When the evening came, I felt calmly in control. Tomorrow, I will start my period, I thought. Tomorrow, I will start my better life.

After bathing my young son and putting him into his crib, then making sure he was asleep, I retrieved my bottle of turpentine from its hiding place. Next, I went into the kitchen and fetched a glass of water—then a teaspoon. At this point, I hesitated, and questioned: Was it a teaspoon? Perhaps it was a tablespoon? At no time had my mother or aunt mentioned how much turpentine one should take.

I decided upon the tablespoon, because I wanted to make sure it worked.

I measured the turpentine and poured it into my glass of water. I stirred the mixture, and then stirred again. It didn't blend well, and I gave it a final swift stir, and then managed a quick, large gulp. It felt hot in my throat, and difficult to swallow. Another quick, swift stir—an intended quicker gulp—but my throat rebelled and refused to swallow any more.

In my dizzy state, I stumbled into my bedroom and crawled into bed. I immediately went to sleep—I think I went to sleep, but can't be sure. It wasn't sleep in my normal condition, but was something else, something different, something entirely different, for my body had split into two.

I could view my one body as it hovered in the air, and that body viewed my second body on the bed: my two bodies seeing one another.

Oddly, my floating body seemed unconcerned about my condition, but my body on the bed knew something was amiss. My "bed" body urged me to rise, and made me aware that I was in danger of dying if I did not get up immediately.

But I couldn't rise. I didn't have enough energy to sit up, or stand up. However, I had enough energy to inch my legs across the mattress and over the bed edge. Surprisingly, this action caused my bodies to rejoin, but for the briefest of moment before separating again. I realized that expenditure of energy was the key to holding my bodies together. I slid my legs farther and farther over the bed edge, then downward, downward, until my feet found the floor.

At some point I flipped my body, enabling me to curve up and above the mattress, my legs hugging the side, my feet on the floor. In this position I inched along the bed edge . . . walking . . . walking, until I felt well enough to return to bed. As soon as I crawled in and returned to prone position, my body separated again.

I repeated the inching of my legs, the walking around the mattress, and testing of my situation, until finally my body stayed together. I then fell into a deep sleep.

I awakened the next morning to the laughter of my toddler son as he played with toys in his crib. The sun was shining in the window. It was another day. But, I froze because I realized the sun could have illuminated a chillingly different tale that morning. What if I had not awakened? When would my young son have been found? What would the police report record? Would they have found the bottle of turpentine, the empty glass with the tablespoon nearby? Would they have shaken their heads and written "suicide" on their records? Secrets can put you riding upon a sled on black ice, one that puts you into an uncontrollable situation, one that forever stains your memory.

Years later, I Googled turpentine and missed periods, for I wondered if anyone other than OOM women did this. Imagine my surprise when I learned that turpentine was used in the past by lay abortionists and self-abortionists—in douches!! Turpentine used in douches!!! Turpentine taken vaginally—not orally! Neither my mother nor my aunt had mentioned that!! (Word of warning: Never use turpentine orally or vaginally!)

Sex communication should flow easily from mother to daughter. Since sex was treated as an "off the table" secret in my home, I believed it to be shameful.

In this day and age, people would call what I did "aborting a possible pregnancy". I can't say if I did or if I didn't, for I was only a few days late with my period. Yet, being only a few days late filled me with such fear and panic that I was ready to reach for anything. If contraceptive or morning after pills had been available at that time, I would never have had to search for an alternative. To desire each baby that comes into this world is a circumstance many women do not have. Yet, to desire each baby that comes into this world is what every baby deserves!

In 1963 Betty Friedan published *The Feminine Mystique[7]*. During that same period of time, women throughout the United States clamored for equal rights. Pots that had bubbled on front burners of stoves remained in their cupboards as women marched in the streets. In my kitchen, unfortunately, pots still bubbled away on my front burners and on my back burners. In my mind-blocked state, I had not the slightest clue of what equal rights meant.

Growing up in the OOM religion, I was taught that women were second to the men, and the man ruled the house. Never, did I entertain the slightest thought in my brain that my husband and I shared equal power. I was subservient because that's who I was raised to be in the Old Order Mennonite religion.

Six years after the birth of our first son, we had our second son. He was darling and healthy in every way. This planned child arrived in our family at a time when I no longer had to work, but could stay home and raise our two sons.

Since I had no "worldly" family model to emulate, I patterned my early years of marriage and motherhood after the family in "Father Knows

Best." During the day, I played with and took care of my sons, took care of the house, ran chores, and purchased the groceries. Shortly before my husband returned home from work, I transformed from mother to wife. I refreshed my makeup, combed my hair, tidied the house, and prepared a perfect dinner. I timed dishes to be table-ready within ten minutes after my husband walked through the door. Margaret, the wife and mother in the "Father Knows Best" television series, portrayed the sort of woman I now knew, the typical wife in the early sixties.

My husband, put on a "fast track" by DuPont, soon had a management position. We were told to expect relocations every year or two. As it turned out, we lived in twelve locations within twenty years.

These moves forced me to mingle with varied groups of people at a time when my sons were growing up. A large percentage of the women I now met in social settings were educated and had graduated from college.

Thirty years after Betty Friedan wrote her powerful book on women's rights, I moved into present time. It took college and creative writing courses to get there.

"Write about something you know," my writing instructors advised. I knew about my childhood religion best of all—but it was something I knew darkly, for I had been taught to keep much quiet from the world. I soon learned that seeing my words on paper made them less frightening, and they lost much of their controlling power.

In the OOM religious community, artistic freedom was not viewed as cute or valuable. For instance, if a young teenage girl, in her moment of whimsy, changed the color of her covering strings from white to pink, it would be tantamount to a lion entering the community. A fear would rage throughout the community, a fear that would not be quieted until the young girl changed her covering string back to the community's color of white. At that time, the fear of defiance would banish.

Since individuality is out and communal life is in, how does an OOM woman express herself? Having many children makes a woman more valuable. Making the best pie adds value to the woman. And putting up (canning) four-hundred and twenty quarts of applesauce will definitely get you attention, although no one would be imprudent enough to praise you outright for your success.

Men are made more valuable through having many children. Many children mean many hands to help a father work his farm. As more sons are born into the family, a father will often purchase extra acreage, and become wealthier in the process. Since OOM children turn their earnings over to their parents until twenty-one, father-farmers have many years of free labor. Likewise, having many daughters will supply mothers with many years of free housekeepers and babysitters, and girls to work the gardens, tend the chickens, and prepare the meals.

Big families were desired and necessary. My parents had eight children, although they planned to have twelve. My parents had children even after my father was noticeably ill from multiple sclerosis. Parents have their babies at home in the OOM community, with father assisting. However, when my youngest brothers John and Paul were born, mother went to the hospital for their births, father being too ill to assist.

When we moved to the big city, having many children was not financially feasible. My siblings and I, acting according to the dictates of our new world, gave our mother ten grandchildren. Her views regarding having many children for God evolved to the point where she believed parents should limit their family size, and use birth control, accordingly.

PACIFISM

Sticks and stones will break my bones.

But words will never hurt me.

CHAPTER 7

The Peaceful Pilgrim

I opened this book (Chapter 1) with a letter that my youngest brother, Paul, had written to our mother. Dated 1968 would have made Paul twenty-five. when he wrote that he never expected to marry, never would have any children, and considered himself to be a loner for some unknown reason, which he delegated to fate. Paul's letter essentially told his mother that he was gay.

At the time, Mother informed all her children that Paul was homosexual. She didn't understand fully what this meant, for naturally, being homosexual was evil, according to OOM teachings. But she was no longer an OOM, so talked with psychologists in Akron and gained knowledge about what this meant. She accepted and loved Paul for who he was.

I had not known about or read Paul's letter until his untimely death in 2010. Then, as executrix of his estate, I found the letter in Paul's San Francisco apartment. Undoubtedly, mother had returned it to him at some earlier time.

His words, *I do not ever feel degraded, immoral, or sinful whether I am in a stockade or walking through a "red-light district,"* returned me to an early morning in Wilmington, Delaware, in the year 1967, where I lived at the time. There, while hurriedly keeping an eye on the clock, my husband sipped morning coffee while glancing through the newspaper. Soon he'd leave for work.

My first-grade son had finished his breakfast and now gathered his lunchbox, his papers, and his jacket. Soon his school bus would pick him up at the corner.

Still asleep in his crib was my toddler-son, or maybe awake and playing, and since either was a possibility, I cocked an ear toward his room.

Intermittent fluttering within my abdomen reminded me that another baby was on the way.

In the midst of this early morning hustle-bustle, the telephone rang. Startled, I looked at the clock. It was exactly 7AM. Could this be anyone other than my mother, who was normally careful not to call me too early?

When I answered, Mom began with a plea, "Esther May, can you do something for me? I just can't do it myself." She then gave me a telephone number to call, and ended her call with the request: "Don't tell anyone about this."

Of course I made the call, since I'm as obedient as the sun. And, of course, I told no one. But it left me with a dead place inside, a dead place I could ignore during my busy years of childrearing, during the busy years beyond, during the long lengths of time when I wouldn't see Paul face-to-face. But when I did, the dilemma raised its ugly two-sided face: Should I tell? Or, should I not tell? Should I be obedient to Mom, or should I be honest with Paul?

Secrets that cause quicksand to form under one's feet! Would secrets never end?

Paul's long journey to San Francisco began in 1965, when he suddenly vanished from his Akron home, the one he shared with his mother. Mother's anguished condition came through in every syllable. "He hasn't come home for two nights now. He didn't go to school for two days either. And he didn't go to work. None of his friends have seen him; none of us have heard from him. He's gone!" She gasped as she said these last words, and then wailed the next few: "He's gone! He's gone! This has never happened before!"

Paul, my youngest brother, always emotionally fragile and shy, was only twelve when we moved to Akron. He had attended junior high, went on to graduate from high school, and was attending Akron University when this incident occurred. A good student, and frequently on the honor roll, he had majored in math and psychology.

"He took nothing with him," mother's tone understandably desperate. "He took nothing. His keys are still on the table, right where he left them. And his car is still parked in the same position. His clothes are still here, his wallet's here, with his driver's license inside. Even his bank account hasn't been touched." Then, as if to cement his outcome, she added,

"He didn't even take any luggage with him. I don't understand it. I don't understand."

I had to admit all this sounded foreboding, so unlike Paul, to say the least, who was most obedient, reliable, conscientious and quiet, unlike his adventurous, and sometimes "rowdy" siblings. We thought he was content with attending college, and looked forward to getting his degree. In the meantime, he had his part time job at the grocery store, and then returned home every evening for supper and sleep.

On Sundays, Paul studied with a male friend named George at the kitchen table. But that seemed about as far as his social connections went. I didn't even think he had ever dated a girl. But, who could be concerned? Busy with his studies and busy with his work, not dating didn't seem unusual for a lad of his age.

But maybe all this meant Paul was gay. Did I know? Did I care? Certainly not! But the real question was, did Paul care? Did he think gayness was an unacceptable condition, considering his upbringing, considering his mother's thoughts in this area? Did he care that he was gay?

However, at the time Paul disappeared, we focused on how to find Paul. "When did you last see him?" I asked mother, then followed with a strong statement, "Did you call the police?"

"Yes!" her voice broke at this point. I heard quick sniffles, then a blow into her hanky. "Yes," she inhaled, deeply, "Yes I did." Her deep inhalation spoke volumes.

"They said he's twenty-one," she continued. "They said this sort of thing happens all the time. A young boy tires of his home circumstances and disappears."

More sniffles, more blowing into her hanky, then mother continued, her voice openly wailing at this point: "They don't know my Paul. He would never do this!"

I felt sorry for her, and had to admit this bizarre behavior was unusual for Paul. To leave without his wallet, and leave without the car he loved—to be gone for a few days—all seemed a stomach turner. Clearly something was wrong!

Trying to be helpful, I suggested she call my husband's uncle, who was a detective on the Akron police force. She called and a brief investigation ensued. The detective-uncle basically reiterated what the police had told her, "Look, some people want to disappear. It happens all the time. Leave him alone."

"But, you don't understand. Paul would never do this." Mother's sniffles into her hanky could be clearly heard over the phone. "I know something's wrong."

Something was wrong. The dates tallied up a story that began with a disappearance from a kitchen table, and spiraled into an appearance in a stockade.

*   *   *

June 11, 1965: The twenty-one year old Paul, living with his mother in her Akron apartment home, finished breakfast about 8 am. He picked up his school books and walked out the door. So far, this was normal behavior. But he never returned home from school that day.

For a full and agonizing forty-nine days, Paul's family searched for him, talked to detectives, worried, asking anyone and everyone if they had seen Paul, heard from him. But not one person had.

July 30, 1965: Six weeks later. A letter arrived from Paul, postmarked from Hermosa Beach, California.

My mother questioned, "Where is that?" In her typical style, she looked up the location in her Atlas. Her question then became: "Why is he there?" And, "How did he get there?" Then followed her most important question: "How can we get him home again?"

In the early sixties when the Vietnam War raged, boys received draft deferments as long as they were in college. Upon leaving, however, your "draft ball" started rolling. It was your duty to notify your controlling board.

In the summer of 1965, President Lyndon Johnson escalated our military presence in Vietnam. Draft calls doubled. He petitioned Congress for additional billions of dollars to support the war.

Paul, being a recent college student, would certainly have been aware of what was going on. Now, with his deferment rights over, he alerted the Draft Board to his new status.

August 29, 1966: Paul enlisted with the Air Force, signing on for a four-year period.

November 21, 1966: Paul's stint with the Air Force didn't last long. Paul went AWOL on this date.

March 15, 1967: On the morning of Mom's phone call to me, I, unknowingly, initiated Paul's arrest in New York City. It happened within the hour of my call. He was taken to an Air Force facility in New Jersey where he was confined to the stockade.

*   *   *

Over the years Paul would say to me, "I wonder who made the call."

At other times Paul would say, "I think it was George. I gave him my address so he could mail me a letter. I'm positive it was him."

At other times, he would tell me how it all went down: "I was staying in an apartment with Bob. He was still sleeping, but I was up in the kitchen making coffee because I had to go to work. I heard sirens, and looked out the window, which gave me a clear view of the street below. I saw the police pull up. I knew they were coming for me."

A second AWOL from the Air Force in 1968 sealed Paul's fate. And for that, he received a Bad Conduct discharge.

Then, on October 4, 1968, the twenty-five-year-old Paul wrote a letter to Mom—as copied in chapter one of this book. His letter mentions his familiarity with stockades and red-light districts.

Did Paul dissociate? Certainly he would have been a candidate for this condition, where acts and behaviors, antagonistic to what one has been taught, can be blocked from the conscious mind. Could that be why he left Mom's apartment, initially?

Old Order Mennonites know nothing of the laws of the land. They fear courts, fear lie detectors, and fear anything that would make them swear in a court. Throughout Paul's interrogation and subsequent court hearings, Paul obeyed what he had been taught. He said nothing to defend his actions, which would be typical of the non-confrontational pilgrim, who has learned to be passive.

In Paul's later years, I asked him why he had left home abruptly. He said he didn't remember making the decision to leave home. He didn't remember leaving, didn't know how he journeyed from his home to the bus, didn't remember actually getting on the bus, and didn't remember traveling at all. He described all memory connected with these events as "black".

However, he remembered arriving in New York City, remembered disembarking the bus in Manhattan, and remembered finding himself car-less, money-less, and identification-less. The few coins that jiggled in his pocket warmed his leg, but, otherwise, he had nothing.

He survived his first day in Manhattan by washing dishes for a restaurant. He survived his first night by sleeping on a subway train. Homeless and practically penniless, he spent his first few months repeating this pattern.

He made friends in Manhattan, and then traveled with them to Chicago, and on to Los Angeles. In Los Angeles, something awakened within him, reminding him of his need to contact the Draft Board. Did he read something in the newspapers? Did his friends advise him of this need? I do not know this answer.

After Paul's discharge from the Air Force, he returned to New York City for a few years, and then on to San Francisco. In this Bay City, Paul met his life partner, a gentleman who, a little older than he, had recently retired from the Air Force and was anxious to travel. He asked Paul to join him.

Paul readily accepted, most open to this sort of adventure, as he was intelligent, college educated, and had been culturally starved by his highly-censored religious youth.

During his travel years with his partner, Paul became a gifted photographer. He won prizes, and eventually had a photo, one which he entitled "Dreamworld", published in the August 1991 issue of *Popular Photography.*

After returning to San Francisco, Paul and his partner cared for feral cats. The cats they cared for inhabited the rocky shoreline along the Bay in Burlingame—a small town situated a little south of the airport, just off the 101 freeway.

Paul and his partner rented a two-bedroom apartment on Pine Street in San Francisco, but the apartment owners didn't allow cats. Paul fell in love with six feral kittens, however, and the kittens mewed and mewed in loving response. Soon the apartment manager rapped on their door. Paul and his partner quietly made a deal with apartment owners, whereby Paul would clean vacated apartments if they'd allow him to keep his kittens. The kittens mewed and played happily for years, maturing into full-grown, contented and healthy cats. Meanwhile, the apartment owners ignored it all.

The arrangement proved happy and satisfying for all. Then, one by one, the cats died. A few years later, Paul's partner died. Then, on the morning of May 15th in 2010, Paul died.

On that fateful morning, Paul followed his customary habit of walking from Pine Street to Larkin Street, to the nearby San Francisco Main

Public Library. It was a nice walk of a little over a mile. He emailed his siblings, using the library's public computers. Since photography had been a highlight of his life, he searched internet sites. Photographs of cats and Old Order Mennonite and Amish people were sites he frequented. He forwarded these pictures on to his siblings.

As computer use at libraries is timed, at some point Paul would have had to relinquish his seat. His usual habit was to browse through book shelves at this point, selecting books of interest, finding a nearby comfortable chair, and losing himself in the pages. In early afternoon he'd head for home, sometimes stopping for a quick cup of decaffeinated coffee and a sweet, custard-filled donut. He then would have hurried home to where his true loves awaited, which, at this time were his two feral-feral cats.

I do not know everything Paul may have done on his last fateful morning here upon this earth, but a few things are certain. He emailed his siblings about ten that morning. The police report stated he died shortly before noon. Therefore, I surmise the following:

Paul probably felt sick and decided to return home. He made it to Pine Street where his apartment was located. A lady on a bus traveling down Pine Street made a 911 call. "A man collapsed onto the sidewalk," she reported. Help soon arrived. Attendants worked on Paul, then transported him to the nearby St. Francis Hospital, but it was too late. An autopsy showed he had a heart attack due to untreated hypertension and was dead upon arrival at the hospital.

Meanwhile, back in Paul's apartment, his two cats meowed and played as they awaited his return. At his first pang of pain, I'm sure Paul thought of his cats. Must get home . . . must get home . . . he would have thought. Push harder, hurry faster . . . faster . . . one more block . . . nearly there . . . have to reach them . . . nearly there. He nearly made it, dying one short block away.

Feral cats, the cats Paul and his partner initially owned, had human contact when kittens—and then were abandoned. Feral cats can be tamed to make good pets. But the two feral-feral cats that awaited Paul's arrival, had been born in the wild and would never make good pets. Yet Paul loved them and cared for them as if they were his children.

Cats come in litters, six or eight at a time. A litter is nothing for mother cat to handle. As the kittens mature, however, a litter will overwhelm cat owners. To ease their stress, cat owners abandon their kittens in undesirable places, hoping their kittens will find a safe hiding place where they can fend for themselves. The deserted shorelines found in Burlingame offered such places.

Paul was born the youngest of eight children. In cat terms, eight would be a litter. Due to Papa's illness of multiple sclerosis, Papa was unable to do much of the farm and garden work, and was unable to handle the workload of raising many children. Overburdened, mother sent most of her children out to work for neighbors. We would be gone for the week, and then would return for the weekend. How much work can a child of seven or eight do? It's more likely that placing us in other's homes eased our mother's burden, much as cat owners ease their burden by abandoning their kittens.

It's the nature of a child to want to play, and not have to work for neighbors. With sour faces we left our home on Monday morning, and then returned with happy faces on Friday evening.

For our work, we earned a few coins, about ten cents for the week, which we promptly turned over to mother. These coins helped her care for her large family. In today's world, such deeds would be deemed child labor—and highly frowned upon. For us, however, with each child contributing a little to our family's financial pot, we were able to stay together.

Highly protected from the beginning, Mother never sent Paul out to work, but kept him home. You would think all this would have made Paul feel loved and valued, would have made him feel "special", and would have made him purr like a petted cat. And that his siblings would have been the ones who felt like abandoned "feral" cats.

The opposite happened. Paul felt guilty that he was not sent out to do his fair share, felt his siblings should hate him, and felt he was the abandoned "feral" cat. It's no wonder Paul related so closely with the forlorn, with the cats who meowed loudly for their food—but skittered into the rocks as soon as someone appeared—hiding—afraid of people—pretending not to exist. Such were the forlorn, feral cats that inhabited the Bay in Burlingame—the cats that Paul related to, and loved.

Paul, the youngest of eight, was perfectly happy living in the shadows of life. He loved being a servant to his feral cats, and never lifted his voice loud enough to ever be a master of anyone in this world. Nonetheless, he had been raised in a religion that embraced elitism. Paul didn't seem to buy into many of their tenets.

Elitism in religion is the belief that God favors me and my particular brand of religion above all others. And, because of my elitist belief, I have the right; indeed, I have the duty to bear many children for God and His church. Such a mission is not easily resisted, for it matches our evolutionary desire to propel our genes forward into the next generation.

Religious elitism has caused wars between neighbors, between villages, between countries, and between cultures for millenniums. Wars change cultures, which changes whose genes will go forward. The winner holds his flag high as he parades his horse across the pulverized landscape. He marches into cities, where he is highly acclaimed. He is invited into the parlors of the wealthy, the prominent, the kings and queens, where he partakes of their best wines and sleeps with their best daughters, all guaranteeing that perceived best genes, those of the intellectual wealthy and those of the strong warrior, will propagate the next generation. Is this not the story recorded in history books and imbedded in many beloved tales?

Although Old Order Mennonites are strong adherents of religious elitism, they are also strong adherents of the doctrine of strict pacifism. Their refusal to fight in a war means their genes will stay home. Their sons and daughters will marry one another, and their genes will live to populate their next generation.

Being born in the United States of America guarantees all citizens the right of religious freedom. This right protects the Old Order Mennonites and their sister religions from ever having to fight in wars, or from even having to support any war that their country declares.

While these religions refuse involvement in secular activities, such as running for office or voting in elections; and while they refuse to accept government monies for health care, education, farm subsidies, and other government-sponsored programs, they faithfully pay their local and federal taxes.

Because the Old Order Mennonites choose to take care of themselves and those within their community, federal and state social workers and health care workers do not come into their community, which facilitates their strict isolationist policies.

Old Order Mennonites believe it is wrong to ever take the life of another human, even if ordered by their government. They have sat peacefully in prisons during wartimes, as a testament to their belief.

My brothers arrived at draft age in the 1950's and '60's. At that time, Mennonite boys registered as Conscientious Objectors, and served their country in peaceful settings. Such service often involved working as orderlies in nearby hospitals. These hospitals could not be affiliated with the Armed Forces in any way. Since we now have an all-volunteer armed force, the draft is no longer a dilemma for Mennonites.

As I've mentioned earlier, within my own pilgrim family, my oldest brother, Mark, arrived at draft age and registered as a Conscientious

Objector. He served his required two years as an orderly in a Cleveland hospital. As long as we were in the Mennonite community, no difficulties arose when registering as an "Objector".

Upon moving to Akron, everything changed for my three younger brothers, Frank, John and Paul, who were fifteen, fourteen and twelve, at the time. Soon, Frank reached the age of sixteen. Since he was no longer a Mennonite, he could no longer register as a Conscientious Objector.

Moving to Akron meant we moved from past to present. Because of timing, some of my siblings arrived there in better condition than others. Frank, the fifth child in our family, was at the cusp. He arrived in Akron in an angry condition.

When a mere child of eight, Frank began working for neighbors, staying from Monday through Friday, then returning home for the weekend. The work Frank did when a boy, was the work required of a man.

Frank, obedient to Old Order Mennonite rules, did poorly in school. As a result, he failed two grades.

Perhaps, his greatest source of anger was that he was bullied by his classmates. Obediently, he remained non-confrontational, and "stood there and took it," as mother had instructed her children to do.

Although teased about his denim overalls, his sugar-bowl haircut, his black, rounded-crown hat, which his oppressors tossed into the air while they laughed and danced and had fun at his expense, he could never utter one word or swing one arm in his defense. The confining rule of non-confrontation bound his arms, his legs, his mouth, but not his rage, which flamed unseen within him.

When Frank reached draft age, he was ready to confront. He viewed the Air Force as a relief-valve tool. He would shoot down every enemy plane he saw as a surrogate to alleviate his anger. Finally, perhaps, he could reset his life to normal. The Air Force, however, rejected his application, not because of his anger, which they never saw, but because of his bad eyes.

"Stick and stones will break my bones, but words will never hurt me," is an axiom familiar to most. Naturally, words can and do injure, and can and do inflict lifelong wounds, as the bullying Frank and my brothers endured in school.

Next in the line of siblings was my brother John, who had been farmed out as well, maybe as early as a seven-year-old. Fortunately, he worked for a man and woman who had no children of their own. They treated him as if he was their son. John didn't attend Columbiana school while working for these folks because he lived in another district. John, an extremely brilliant boy, still obeyed his mother's instruction, and tried to get bad grades.

When John arrived at the age when a boy must register for service, he selected the National Guard Reserve.

As mentioned earlier, Paul, my youngest brother, was never farmed out to neighbors. And, because of timing, he never tried to get bad grades. After graduating from Akron's North High, he enrolled in college, which gave him a deferment for as long as he attended school. All ended when he escaped to New York City. Paul selected the Air Force as his preferred choice, possibly following his older brother's choice.

Years after my bashful brother Paul went AWOL from the Air Force, I asked him if he had told the Air Force that he had been brought up as an Old Order Mennonite. My thinking was that surely this bit of information would have benefited Paul. Would not strong, pacifist teachings offer some defense of his behavior?

Paul said, "No, I never told them." Of course that would be true. Paul did as we all did, and faithfully kept the OOM secret: *Don't tell anyone about our religion!*

Paul couldn't handle confinement, the opposite of freedom. And who could blame him? At least I had some relief while growing up. I was fortunate enough to work for non-Mennonites at times, and viewed these work stints as great diversions from my confining home. I experienced my first radio program and had my first brush with television while working for non-Mennonite people. And I learned what Old Order Mennonites termed as "evil things of the world" were actually good. These diversions, or escapes, eased my entrance into the world when we moved.

Paul simply didn't have an opportunity to escape, for, protected as he was by mother, he was never sent out to work for neighbors or non-Mennonites.

Confrontation, whether by stick, stones, or words, activates the fight or flight centers of the hypothalamus. When one, such as the Old Order Mennonite child and adult, is not allowed to fight back, but must stand there and take it, one is rendered defenseless. A defenseless person has no control over his or her life and becomes passive, childlike, which exactly describes an Old Order Mennonite. Passive people are not adventurous, do not search out and taste other opportunities, but tend to remain within their fold.

My mother rose above her passivity and became dynamic when she told church officials, "I can't live on man-made rules anymore." She remained strong enough to get her children out as well. Does this mean we were finally able to defend ourselves and become aggressive? It did not. And it did not for mother, either.

As my mother struggled to speak publicly, most of my siblings have had to battle this terror, as well. We took public speaking courses offered by Dale Carnegie and Toastmaster. Even though we knew we had something valuable to say, we'd stumble through our speeches in a frozen condition. Our stress over public speaking was too great, and we'd finally give up trying.

I've taken public speaking courses twice, and took as many as I could when in college. To combat my fear, I memorized my entire speech. Memorizing the speech put me into robot form, which enabled me to deliver my speech in a different body. Audiences are never fooled. They want the real you.

Most people view the OOM, and those of our sister religions, as void of anger. I'd say the OOM have been taught to swallow anger. Anger swallowed does not get digested, but gets belched from time to time. The results on your hanky are not pretty, to say the least.

In our religion we were taught to go to the dark closet and pray to God when stressors became unbearable. God could help us through our times of need, we were counseled. This amounted to shifting your troubles onto God's shoulders. He's good and He's big, and He can handle them. However, it's the passive way of handling stress—and never fixes the cause of your troubles.

When *Rolling Down Black Stockings* was published, readers asked me if I was angry about what happened to me because of my childhood religion. I admitted that, after writing my memoir, I cried for weeks about the hurt that mother and father had endured, and the hurt that my siblings and I endured as well—all because of an oppressive religion. I didn't react in anger, but in sadness, for I didn't blame the Old Order Mennonites for what happened to us. Those who are harmed will harm, unless taught a different way. And those who live within an isolated community, and have a limited education, will never know a different way.

In extreme religions, tensions among individual members can be as taut as a stretched rubber band. An individual, always a man, will perceive injustice and snap. He convinces family members of this injustice and they'll snap with him. In my own family situation, you might say that my mother snapped. She was labeled mentally unstable by the OOMs.

My mother hated the bickering that OOM's typically do. In my childhood, when community members came around, complaining that so-and-so had done such-and-such, mother patiently listened. As soon as they left, she threw her hands up into the air, and said, "Peace, peace, all I want is peace."

Old Order Mennonites confront, or speak up for themselves, when perceived injustices about a community member or members become unbearable. "I must speak to a bishop," they'll say at such times. "I can't live this way anymore. A bishop or elder will do something about this."

Sometimes the only way a dispute can be settled is through a schism. Schisms are non-confrontational, which means no one is allowed to have an all-out word war or fist fight. No one is declared the winner and no one is declared the loser. Although no physical contacts are made, the hurt feelings and grudges are remembered for decades. "Well, you know when your great-grandfather fussed about my great-grandfather's insistence that our women wear their skirts ankle length. Your great-grandfather was wrong. No sense in skirts being any higher then, and no sense in skirts being any higher now!"

In severe schisms, a family (generally several families) or groups of members, who disagree with a bishop's dictum, or disagree with some aspect of the religion, pick up *en masse* and leave. They'll start another church settlement on their own, which could be nearby, or as far away as Canada, Mexico, or a South American country. These migrations are beneficial, for they plant pockets of Mennonites in various isolated locations, where they thrive by working off the land.

Schisms have another benefit for the OOM religion as well, for it keeps church communities small and easily managed. It also opens opportunities for power-seeking males, who froth upon the surface of a seemingly peaceful community. Not easily contained, these males spread discontent of one sort or another until they have power and control. Man is man, and gene is gene, no matter what outward façade you choose to wear.

Hutterities have long known that a power-hungry male's discontent needs relief, and that spreading leadership to many, rather than bestowing leadership upon a few, is the recipe for peace. Therefore, when a Hutterite community, or colony as more commonly called, grows to more than a hundred, a few men are chosen to seed a new colony. They also choose the women who will populate their new colony. The women, subjugated as they are, have no choice in this colony-selecting process. Generally, a Hutterite woman is groomed to want children. And moving to a new colony almost guarantees that she'll get a husband.

Within a culture, community and religion, deactivating the "fight" response is more easily accomplished by some than by others. This was true within my childhood community as well, even though our religion had harsh non-confrontation rules.

Babies, in all cultures, greet the world with their own distinctive personalities: Some are born passive and rarely cry—while others fight off any bootie or mitten placed on their tiny feet or hands. Some smile at the slightest sensation—while others take a great deal of coaxing to give up a slightest curl of lip. Some are born testy—while others arrive with a most gentle spirit.

In my family, not all of my siblings were born with Paul's gentle spirit. In fact, not all of my siblings had his absolute love of cats. On one summer afternoon, my heck sister witnessed our pet cat kill a baby chick. My siblings and I, who were present at the time, thought it no worse than our cat killing a mouse.

But not Heck! Heck was not of this orientation, and suddenly burst upon the scene with a baseball bat in hand. Before we knew what was happening, she struck our pet cat on the head with such ferocity that it popped out the cat's eye. Naturally, it killed the cat instantly.

So much for Heck's non-confrontation teachings! And so much for deactivating Heck's "fight" response! When questioned, Heck merely offered this excuse, "I got so mad, my mind went black."

As any cat owner knows, it's impossible to catch an unaware cat. It boggles the mind to learn that someone could rush toward a cat with a baseball bat in hand. And it's even more unbelievable to know that someone could strike that cat on the head and deliver a fatal blow. Yet, my heck sister did all that, proving she was faster than a cat.

Another sibling, at age ten, recounted how, in a fit of anger, he stuck a live chick up a drain pipe and left the poor thing there to die. He admitted his anger was misplaced, for the poor chick had done nothing wrong, but merely served as a handy object upon which to vent his rage. The real individual, a grownup, who had caused his great anger wasn't at hand—or maybe, wouldn't be as easy to handle. Furthermore, it's hard to stick a grown person up a drain pipe.

These two confrontational incidents involved animals within easy reach, and with some familiarity. After all, if you've grown up on a farm, you get used to killing animals. And the Bible doesn't say: *Thou shalt not kill animals*. It only says: *Thou shalt not kill*.

It's worth noting that none of my siblings has ever murdered a person, or caused any bodily harm to another person because of anger. Praise the Old Order Mennonite's non-confrontation doctrine for this!

Then, again, perhaps OOMs should not be praised for their stringent non-confrontation doctrine for it renders martyrs, not murderers. It renders martyrs who cannot even defend themselves when struck with fists or words, but must stand there and take it. So much for choices!

After writing *Rolling Down Black Stockings*, I began questioning the non-confrontation policy of my childhood religion, and especially their "turn the other cheek" doctrine. Mennonites are known as peaceful people, almost without anger, but I know them to have great anger at times. I've seen milk stools fly through the air and strike wooden stalls. And I've seen milk stools picked up and whacked against an innocent cow's rump over and over again. I've seen pigs stuck with pitchforks, repeatedly, for stubbornly refusing to go into their pens. But, I have never witnessed out-of-control violence directed at a human being with such force that it resulted in a homicide case.

My questioning led me to read Lonnie Athens' book, *Violent Criminal Acts and Actors*[8]. And Athens' book led me to Richard Rhodes' book: *Why They Kill*[9]. Both books discuss the subject of violent behaviors with extreme insightfulness.

Richard Rhodes' book, *Why They Kill*, consists of three parts. Part 1 tells Lonnie Athens' story, his childhood, and Lonnie's choice of vocation. (Basically, Lonnie conducted interviews with hardened criminals, and speculated as to why these individuals had committed crimes.)

In Part 2, Richard Rhodes tests Lonnie Athens' hypothesis on some of Athens' well-documented, high-profile cases, such as the Lee Harvey Oswald case, the Cheryl Crane case, and others.

In Part 3, Rhodes writes about preparations for war, and then discusses and details the many aspects of medieval brutalization.

Rhodes says that within each of us resides a phantom ghost. We acquire our phantom ghost in childhood when we experience violent situations, and we learn through these experiences. When we are threatened, our phantom ghost speaks to us and guides our behavior.

Rhodes' concept of a phantom ghost residing within us makes sense. I think it could even be called "imprinting". These ghosts develop when we are children and witness how anger is handled in dangerous situations.

Since the Old Order Mennonites are pacifists, I wondered how Rhodes' phantom-ghost theory fits into their doctrine. Do peaceful Old Order Mennonites have peaceful phantom ghosts residing within them?

Yes, they do!

OOM children have never witnessed violent behavior against humans, such as a shooting, a knifing, or even angry or hateful words used like swords directed at others. They have never served in war. Books and literature involving violent behavior were banned. Although we knew the Bible's Old Testament contained much violent behavior in war stories, and stories such as Cain and Abel, we were taught that we should follow the New Testament. Jesus initiated the peaceful way of handling anger when he told his followers that if someone slapped you on one cheek, give up your other cheek, as well.

In *Violent Criminal Acts and Actors*, author Lonnie Athens lists the causes of criminal acts in four categories: (1) Self defense; (2) Frustration when a victim is unwilling to go along with the perpetrator's desires; (3) Hatred of a person (victim) who is viewed as evil; and (4) Frustration with the victim's conduct, which the perpetrator judges as intolerable.

The peaceful OOM relates to these four behavioral categories as follows:

(1) Self defense. Old Order Mennonites have a strong non-confrontation doctrine. As children, if we struck a sibling or other playmate in dispute, we were immediately scolded or spanked. Fearful of the punishment, we did not engage in violent behaviors.

Anger is anger, however, and cannot be defused by punishment. Indeed, punishment, normally, causes an increase in anger. Anger can sometimes be diminished through sneaky behavior, when one retaliates without the offender's awareness.

I offer myself as an example. When I, as a child, felt a sibling had offended me, I retaliated in a sneaky, non-violent way. I licked the offender's plate as I set the table for supper. This action might make you gag or laugh about it, but it eased my anger, for I felt I had righted a wrong.

In *Rolling Down Black Stockings* I wrote that my sister Sarah handled a perceived injustice by throwing my doll baby into the furnace fire. Symbolically, this was murder. Naturally, Sarah was punished for her violent behavior when made to surrender *her* baby doll to me. All girls know an exchange of dolls will not work in a child's world. Solomon would not have settled this dispute in such a way.

(2) Lonnie's second category: frustration because others will not go along with the perpetrator's desires, happens simply because there are as many different personalities in one's circle of acquaintances as there are varieties of Campbell's soup.

In my childhood I witnessed a fist fight which continued to the point where bystanders had to step in and physically separate the frustrated perpetrators. Other than this rare fistfight, I never witnessed a physical confrontation.

As children, a "strike them back" or a "go-out-and-get-them" mentality never existed as a way of resolving conflict within our culture.

(3) Hatred of a person viewed as evil—and

(4) Frustration with the victim's intolerable conduct. Both 3 and 4 deal with the punishment of others viewed as evil.

Passing judgment on one another, discerning what is good or bad, are traits thought of as belonging to God. However, as long as humans have existed, they have viewed such traits as their inherited right. Rightfully, this should be true since we have been taught that we are God's children.

As I have experienced in my growing-up years within their community, Old Order Mennonites are extremely inflexible, and tend to see their world in only black-or-white terms. Therefore, it would seem that Lonnie's "punishing others when evil" category would conflict with their passionate non-confrontation belief. At first blush this is true.

An Old Order Mennonite is quick to pronounce rightful justification for denouncing everything and anything viewed as evil. They seem to have perfected the art of slicing one's arm through the air with the finest of flair. Accompanied are strong statements, such as, "It's bad! It's evil! It should not happen!" Such actions and statements are climaxed with finality, "And you can tell anybody you want to that I said so!"

Other than slicing through the air, which might be seen as a symbol of violence, no one is caused physical harm.

No one in the community ever thinks of taking violence to the next level, like blowing up a neighbor's house, or blowing up the neighboring town. In fact, no one believes they have the right to wipe out an evil person in any violent way. Instead, we were taught that God will punish the evil people and throw them into hell. We were to maintain our peaceful ways, our hands tied with non-confrontational tape.

Throughout the ages people have learned peaceful ways to right wrongs. Some of these ways are through charitable gifts, barn-raisings, by joining choral groups, through singing hymns at home, by attending Sunday social dinners, and, by following Martin Luther King's example in which he righted a wrong by creating and leading a great cause in a peaceful way.

Emotional stoicism, where you appear as if made of stone, is nothing more and nothing less than a personal fortified façade. Generally, stoicism sufficiently conceals great anger. When anger festers to the point that one becomes a boiling pot, a doctor can be visited to obtain "nerve" pills, as mother called them.

Within our community, health complaints flourished, particularly among the women. Fringe treatments became common topics, as common as latest fashions discussed by women of the world. And, fringe treatments were frequently utilized. Today, OOM and Amish communities still utilize such treatments, as they travel to Montana, near Helena, and stand in uranium mines for health purposes.

Naturally, the alternative treatment in Colorado utilized by my mother could be considered a fringe treatment. But it turned her life around, and turned the lives of my siblings and myself around, as well. Her alternative treatment consisted of diets and fruit juices, and a step out of isolation, which probably did her the most good in the long run.

Old Order Mennonites have depression, which they view as unsettling, something not well understood. Going to your dark closet and praying was the encouraged way of relief. If prayer doesn't help, a doctor could be consulted.

At times a doctor would send the depressed individual to a psychiatrist or psychologist. The need to see a "doctor of the head" is frightening to most people brought up in the OOM religion. Naturally, the fear was that a head doctor might see one of those secrets stored within.

My oldest brother Mark talks about how his psychiatrist, a woman, wanted to hypnotize him at one point. He laughs, and then says, "She tried it. It didn't happen. She never could put me under."

I know depression as well, the fear of doctors, the inability to reveal what was in my head.

At thirty-one, and having lived in the City for nearly fifteen years, I experienced a major depressive episode. I was married and the mother of two wonderful young sons at the time. A move to a new location placed me in a country situation, where I found myself living in isolation, much like I had in my childhood.

Gloom came suddenly, seemingly overnight, and I found myself in another world. I've heard some describe this other world as a dark forest, which seems appropriate. I could see my husband and children on the outside, but couldn't reach them. Outward signs of depression were everywhere: I had bouts of immense energy, followed with bouts of overwhelming exhaustion. During bouts of energy, I baked cookies of all sorts. Cookies cluttered the kitchen table and counter tops; cookies filled the refrigerator and freezer. In down times, I collapsed into crying episodes, and became non-functional.

Sleep came in bouts as well: my days and nights lacked order. Then, fortunately, I found a lump in my throat. I couldn't swallow without conscious effort and was sure I had cancer. Frantic fear that I would die sent me to a doctor.

A thin, pale, young woman presented herself at the doctor's office on that day, a woman convinced she had cancer. The doctor looked at me, and then calmly said, "I don't think you have cancer, but I'll check you just the same." After a brief physical examination, he said, "I'm sure you don't have cancer." Then he wheeled his chair around and looked directly into my face. "Now," he said, with utmost sincerity and kindness, "why don't you tell me what's really wrong."

Startled, I answered, "N-n-nothing. N-n-nothing's wrong. I thought I had cancer, that's all."

"You don't have cancer," my doctor assured. "When you get ready to talk, come back, and I'll be here to listen. In the meantime I'll prescribe some Valium for you. I think these will help."

The Valium pills turned my condition around within the hour. I could eat, sleep, and the lump in my throat was gone. As for going back to that doctor for the talk, the thought was enough to set my nerve endings aflame. What would I say to him? I wondered.

Although I could not tell this to my doctor, some things I did know. For instance, I knew I had been looking out our front window of my living room lately. And I knew that I watched trucks as they passed by. And I knew that I had timed them—and I knew how many seconds it took for a truck to appear at the top of the hill, and then pass by my front window. I knew a truck driver would never have had time to stop, should a body be lying on the road. I knew all this, but never returned for that talk.

Amazingly, my Valium pill, like my valium hymns, eased my depression.

The Christian religion teaches that everyone is born into the world with a fatal flaw, and that flaw is evil. In order to be redeemed, or made good in the eyes of God, one must acknowledge Jesus Christ as one's Savior. The evil part of you will then be cleansed and all will be forgiven.

Baptism is the representation of washing away this fatal flaw, or sin one is born with. Certainly, logic would question why a perfect God would create humans with a fatal flaw in the first place.

Wars are initiated and fought, even after one becomes a Christian. Wars are easier to understand when viewed through biological eyes, for wars can then be seen as evolution-in-action. Only the fittest governments, cultures, and societies will survive because they have proven evolution's requirement.

Even wars fought to wipe out evil because of elitist reasons, such as we are good and you are bad, can be classified as a biological evolutionary event, or a survival-of-the fittest event. Only genes that survive will live on to populate the next generation.

Even wars fought for economic reasons result in a shuffling of fortunes, and can be viewed as biological evolutionary events. The winner's genes will live on and prosper in the days, months, years, and centuries that follow.

Old Order Mennonites do not believe in evolution, although pacifism is heartily embraced. Disputes are settled through schisms, which is evolution-in-action. No one dies in a schism, and both groups can be declared winners in the "survival of the fittest" contest. New communities are formed. Each group now freely and generously populates their next generations.

As I began this chapter, my youngest brother Paul had died on a San Francisco sidewalk. As a result, two of my siblings, Ruth and Frank, have joined me in this big city nestled between the Pacific Ocean and San Francisco Bay. Paul lived on Pine Street, within walking distance to Market Street, to Main, to Mission, to Lombard, to the enchanting Embarcadero, and to the grand Golden Gate Park. If he wished, he could take a whimsical trolley to China Town, to Japan Town, to downtown, to wherever his heart desired. Paul had lived there for thirty-plus years and loved his multi-varied city.

Earlier in the day, Ruth, Frank and I had identified our dear brother's body at the city morgue. He lay facing upward, as if in a straightjacket, something he started his life wearing, but had tried to shed when in his early twenties.

"It's Paul," we confirmed, wishing they had turned his head toward us. We wanted to see his face one last time, his beautiful, serene face. Undoubtedly, at this point, his face would have said, "Don't worry about me! Worry about my cats!"

After leaving the morgue, we visited a local funeral home to make preparations for cremation of Paul's body. The next order of the day was to visit Paul's apartment.

"The door has been yellow-taped," the policeman informed us after we had identified the body. He gave us the key to the apartment, which they found on him when he died.

"No one has been allowed to enter the apartment since we taped it," the policeman assured. "But you can now remove the tape and go in."

The policeman reported more, "He didn't have much on him when he died, just this key, his driver's license, and a small amount of pocket money. That's all he had on him."

We could have added: "That's more than he had on him when he began his long AWOL journey. First, he left his Akron home, and then he left the Air Force. We were shocked when he left home, but not the latter. For we knew that Paul, always kind and gentle, and raised to be non-confrontational to the extreme, could not have long endured in the Air Force's harsh Vietnam War days.

The police had initially visited Paul's apartment because he had no contact papers on him when he died. They talked with the apartment manager, who warned: "There's two cats in that apartment, and they are both wild. You had better be prepared."

As she had warned the police, these cats were wild. During our previous visits with Paul, we had never seen the cats. Instead, we had settled for wild eyes gazing at us from under a bed; for rumbling noises in a closet as the cats vied for best viewing position; for brushing movements against boxes that had been stacked in a corner, for crashing sounds as boxes fell over, sending cats, like shooting stars, blasting into the air. But, never were we honored with a softest meow that would have offered a slightest clue that cats lived in this apartment.

From what I had experienced during my earlier visits, I could imagine the cats' fright upon seeing the police. They would have hissed, ran, leaped, jumped, and hissed some more. Police have their ways of dealing with hissy cats, however.

As we entered now, we saw battle scars all over the place. Papers littered the tables and floors, a couch cocked awkwardly; chairs stood on their backs with four feet in the air; a refrigerator pulled away from the wall, its yanked plug lying awkwardly nearby. All testified to a humongous contest between the cats and the police.

Although Paul could never battle someone in life, he would have praised his cats for fighting. "Good going!" he would have coached. "Don't let anyone take your freedom away without a good fight!"

But knowing that his cats had lost their last battle would have saddened Paul greatly. The apartment manager informed us that his two cats were taken away and euthanized, probably within a few hours after Paul died, not much longer, they assured.

Not much longer . . . not for long . . . hopefully. For I could take comfort in believing that warm bodies had joined one another on that day, warm bodies in the air . . . joining each other out there . . . joining, before all became cold. And I could see Paul laughing as his cats tumbled toward him, first one, and then the other . . . reaching out . . . jumping in . . . meowing . . . licking . . . meowing . . . licking. I could see this happening out there in the air. I could see this happening before anyone turned cold.

After a satisfying bowl of hot clam chowder, accompanied with a glass of cold chardonnay, we retired to our rooms. We chose the Holiday Inn downtown San Francisco, for it was within walking distance of Paul's apartment. Frank had one hotel room, while Ruth (my heck sister) and I took the adjacent room. I was tired and ready to call it a day, but Heck, always full of nervous energy, wasn't interested in relaxing. Instead, she wanted to talk.

I closed my eyes, pretending to sleep, yet visualized all that transpired. Heck sat on the edge of her bed, her skinny legs draping across the side of the mattress, her feet dangling midway. She seemed deep in thought, yet peeked over at me again and again. I know all this because we are sisters, and I don't need to *see* to *know*.

Since I didn't respond, she began clapping the toes of her sneakers together. *Clap, clap—pause—clap, clap—pause—glare!* I kept my eyes tightly closed, refusing to give in to her claps. So, she repeated it all: *Clap, clap—pause—clap, clap—pause—glare!* Glare! GLARE!

I wanted her shoe-clapping to stop. But most of all, I didn't want to enter into any sort of dialogue with her at this late hour. As usual, she would have taken her superior position in any conversation we conducted, and I'd have to settle for inferior. I didn't need this tonight!

Heck had no intention of allowing me to sleep, so she tried her shoe clapping once again. I chanced the slightest eyelid movement, which she saw in an instant, which caused her to get off her bed and stare into my face. What could I do but open my eyes?

She hopped back onto her bed and began her "superior" conversation: "You know what happens when you die, don't you?" *Clap, clap.*

"What do you mean?" I asked, still basking in the thought that warm bodies could meet up with one another in the air. Her question shook my comfort zone. And I worried about where her conversation was heading. I needed to buy time, but was too exhausted to come up with a response.

Clap, clap—pause—clap, clap. "It's lights out, sister, that's what it is when we die. It's lights out. No more consciousness." *Clap, clap.*

Aroused, okay angered, I asked, "Like what?" Ruth, two years my senior, had always lorded her age over me. "I'm your big sister," she had reminded me over the years. "Listen to your big sister." And, over the years, I had learned that to disagree with Ruth was to lose. As typical, she allowed no pauses.

"It's lights out, kid-do! That's what! Lights out!" Upon saying this, she smacked her hands together in scissors-like fashion, and then repeated, "Lights out!"

"I don't believe that," I said, my voice surprisingly strong, strengthened through irritation. I had had just about enough of her clapping, her smacking, her points-of-view offered in scissor finality.

"I refuse to believe that!" I said. "What happens to energy when we die? Energy can never be created nor destroyed. So, what happens to the energy in our body when we die?"

"I know nuttin' 'bout that," she said, and scissor-smacked her hands again. "All I know is when you're dead, you're dead!"

"Somehow you live on," I countered, bravely. "Somehow energy prevails."

"Dream on, little sister. Dream on. When you're dead, it's lights out. That's all!" She resumed her sneaker clicking to some remote rhythm playing in her head: *two claps, pause, two claps, pause*—repeating again and again.

Through my many years of wandering in the big city, I had learned not to take life too seriously. I had left my black-and-white denunciations behind, and had learned to live in the gray area, the area where peaceful people existed, and where one is not prone to sneaker-clap dangling feet.

With this thought in mind, I offered Ruth a suggestion, "Could you not just learn to row, row your boat? Could you not just go gently down the stream?"

"Merrily, merrily, merrily, merrily, life is but a dream," she finished the lines for me. "See! I'm right!" she pounced back. "Life is but a dream, and then you die. Don't you get it?"

She resumed her clapping of sneakers, then paused long enough to say, "Life is but a dream. Dream on, little sister! Dream on!"

Ruth never caught the non-confrontation, subjugation, and passive doctrines, which has earned her the nickname of "heck" in this book.

The title of this chapter is "The Peaceful Pilgrim"—yet I know a pilgrim can experience great storms internally in times such as these.

Fortunately, since I had been raised to be stoic, I had learned to handle such storms. As my mother instructed, I counted numbers in my head. One, two, three, four—and on to five hundred, five-hundred one, five-hundred two—until my brain cooled and I went to sleep.

If counting numbers had not done the trick, my mother had taught me to recite "proverbs", as she called them. Proverbs relating to anger were as follows:

1. An angry man opens his mouth and shuts his eyes. A peaceful man does the opposite.
2. Be slow to anger; be quick to forgive.
3. It is best *not* to be angry; it's next best to quickly reconcile.
4. Don't worry when you stumble. A worm is about the only thing that doesn't fall.
6. A little humor is the best salve for anger.

Even if a pilgrim doesn't have to dissipate anger, it's good to recite proverbs in one's head. Some of mother's favorites were:

1. Make hay while the sun shines
2. Birds of a feather flock together.
3. A stitch in time saves nine.
4. When you open your mouth, you show who you are.
5. What you wear shows who you are.

Over the years I have learned to write good proverbs as well. Proverbs that describe pilgrim-robots are:

1. Robots make mountains out of molehills.
2. Robots live in a "monkey see, monkey do" world.

Most of my siblings grew up to be passive, as we had been trained. I include myself in their group. But Ruth grew up with a dominant nature. Frankly, a "dominant pilgrim" is an oxymoron, but my heck sister managed to make them mean "cleverly endearing".

I once asked Ruth if she had told anyone about her OOM background when we left the religion, for it seemed to be a commonality with my siblings and myself.

"Oh, no!" she exclaimed. "I was too ashamed. I didn't even tell anyone I had all you brothers and sisters. I was too ashamed of that!"

"That's severe!" I exclaimed.

"I just don't know why I was so ashamed of you all. I'm sorry about it now."

"Don't beat yourself up," I said. "We all were ashamed to tell anyone that we had grown up Old Order Mennonite. It's something that we all didn't do."

THE GOLDEN RULE OF FREEDOM

Live and Let Live

CHAPTER 8

The Perfect Pilgrim

Supper, in my Columbiana house, once meant eating an easily-digested meal. All this ended when I was sixteen, when a small plaque appeared on our kitchen wall, just above our table. This plaque simply read: "Live and let live".

Such unpretentious, alliterative words should have easily slipped through my system, as easily as "Simple Simon, met a pie-man, and "Little Bo Peep has lost her sheep". Instead, these words, confined as they were within the face of a plaque, refused to stay there, and leaped toward me from their place of bondage, and assailed my very essence.

My mother had placed this plaque on the wall earlier that day. Upon returning home from a short shopping trip into the town of Columbiana, she promptly produced a stepladder. Hammering noises were soon heard in the kitchen, followed by words of determination—"There! That's done!"—spoken firmly and resolutely.

The plaque was about the size of a small loaf of bread, and made of white glass that shimmered like sugar. In the upper right and lower left corners were hand-painted bunches of blue forget-me-nots. These flowers had creamy, yellow centers, as creamy and as yellow as the butter on the table.

A silver chain, serving as a frame, surrounded the white glass on all sides, then gathered together and formed a bow at the top. Behind the bow was a loop for hanging.

Centered within the forget-me-nots was shiny, black lettering, painted in fashionable, cursive style. These letters—"Live and Let Live"—were the words that had perplexed me greatly. At the time, I had not the slightest idea of what they meant, or what mother was trying to convey.

Yet, I did know that this plaque shattered most of the rules in our home. We weren't allowed to have decorations on our walls. "Too worldly," our religion had said; "Too worldly," mother had echoed. Indeed, this plaque represented a shocking departure from what had been allowed.

And, somehow these shiny, black words, although nonsensical to me at the time, had meaning and power, the sort of words suddenly positioned upon a new flag, a flag coming out of nowhere, but going somewhere, a flag passing high—passing by—a flag powerful enough to awaken sleeping pilgrims.

"Live and let live" suggests that one should live independently of one another, and not fix restrictive rules on each other. This idea was uncharacteristic of our religious commune. Members in our community functioned as if in one ball. Members promised to help one another. Members promised to watch over one another, no matter what, no matter when. No one in our community lived independently.

Yet, there was my mother's flag, hoisted high, passing by, where all could see, all those who were not asleep with valium hymns, that is. A few months after mother purchased the plaque, she announced we were moving to Akron.

Startled by her announcement, Old Order Mennonites visited mother. "Think about what you're doing!" they said. "Think about what you'll be doing to your children!"

My mother, emboldened by her flag, answered with equally strong words, "Old Order Mennonites believe in too many man-made rules. I believe in the Word of God." She held up her Bible, which she had recently received from Rex Humbard's ministry, and shook the Bible at them. "I intend to follow Full Gospel from now on!" she stated, emphatically.

It's no wonder mother's words were ill-received by the community. She was the passive pilgrim who had always followed the established pathway, and had promised as much when she joined the Mennonite church. She had been taught to hide within the protective folds of her house if revolutionary ideas stirred the air. "Men-folk took care of rebellions," they had said, "and men-folk took care of them without hoisting flags or marching troops or shaking Bibles in the air." For a woman to break away from the protective arms of a man was simply unheard of! Was she insane?

Obviously, mother had lessons to learn when we made the move to Akron, but none was due to insanity. She had lessons to learn because she was a pacesetter, an innovator with bold words that burned within her. As far as she was concerned, "live and let live" made her equal to the man. She was determined to fulfill her dream of being an evangelistic preacher for God.

My siblings and I, on the other hand, had a brightly-lit candle that burned within us as well. It was a timed candle, and tied to our genes.

Arriving in Akron, between the ages of twelve and twenty-two, we arrived as needy teenagers. We dated, married, and learned our new culture through our spouses and our children. Before we moved, we had never known that Easter Bunnies and tooth fairies existed. We were unfamiliar with the tradition of Christmas: Santa Claus, decorated trees, lighted angels, and wreathes on doors. We had lived plainly, and without the countless cultural "accessories" used by people of the world to enhance their lives.

In our new culture, photographs were allowed. Each new event was snapped. Visual remembrances seemed important of how things were at such and such a time, but photographs would last longer. Our generation seemed aware that cultural conditions changed over time, and we were obsessed with documenting all in photos.

In trying to capture our lives through the medium of photographs, we were actually documenting our evolution—in much the same way a tree documents evolution through tree rings. We were simply recording environmental changes through time.

Sometimes there'd be a flurry of photographs, such as at weddings, at the births of our children, at their first days in school, at baseball practice, graduations, etc. All were recorded by cameras, processed, and stored away as photographs. These remembrances became our treasures.

Not all memories are documented through photographs, naturally. Most come from stories we have read or heard about, which are stored as memories in our brains. These memories can be retrieved at our pleasure. Perhaps, strangest of all are the photographic memories that come from our childhood, and are stored in our brain. These memories return so clearly, as if captured on a DVD disc. When played back, they place us in a different locale and time, and return with the emotion we experienced then, as well.

Generally, big events are remembered by all, and documented, which is true with tree rings as well. Moving to Akron, for instance, was a huge event in my life, and in the lives of my family. In fact, it was a game changer in the lives of my siblings and me, and a game changer for the Old Order Mennonite community, as well. For the Old Order Mennonite community, our move could be considered an evolutionary event. Our move to Akron removed suitable partners from their religion's store-shed of available sons and daughters. Since dating outside the religious community was forbidden, removing eight children left them with quite a void.

Life upon this earth begins with our birth. Our pilgrimage plays through until our death. Documenting our lives can be accomplished through many sources. Most families without religious prohibition have boxes and boxes of photographs that document their story. Because of religious prohibition, I have only a photograph or two that captures my mother's years spent as an Old Order Mennonite. My knowledge generally comes from verbal information that has been given to me by family members and acquaintances.

My mother's life pilgrimage began in 1906, in Dayton, Virginia, when she was born as the fourth daughter of Alfred and Amanda (Lehman) Rhodes. She was named Fannie, and had three older sisters named Mary, Minnie, and Annie. Two younger brothers were soon added to the family, with names of Jacob and Joseph.

Because of harsh (environmental) farming conditions in Virginia during my mother's childhood, her parents struggled to make a living for their family. Relatives in Ohio, however, cited excellent growing conditions, and crowed about their prosperous fields of corn, tomatoes and beans. In April of 1913 the family moved from Dayton, Virginia to Columbiana, Ohio, for a better life.

The family traveled by train, selling most of their goods and property beforehand, which would have been expensive to transport by train. With minimal possessions, the family rented a furnished farmhouse in the already established Old Order Mennonite community.

Unfortunately, the family arrived with illness, which the two youngest boys had contracted on the train. Within days upon their arrival, Jacob and Joseph succumbed to their sickness. Both boys were buried in the OOM "White Church" cemetery, at the northernmost end of Germantown Road.

After renting the farmhouse for a few years, my maternal grandparents managed to save enough money to purchase a modest home at the corner of Germantown and Knopp Roads. Perhaps unwilling to chance farming again, they started a chicken hatchery, which provided a nice income for them.

This modest home happened to be an eighth of a mile from where my birth home would eventually be—my Germantown Road bungalow. And my Germantown Road bungalow happened to be an eighth of a mile from my father's family home and farm, the farm that ran the prosperous strawberry business upon which mother was employed as a grasshopper.

A few years after Jacob and Joseph succumbed to their childhood diseases, a fifth daughter, Sarah, was born. A son, John, and a daughter, Hannah, rounded out their family, making nine children altogether: seven living to be adults and two dying in childhood.

Eventually, of the seven surviving children, one never had children, and one adopted a son. The remaining five bore many children, so many that my maternal grandparents eventually had forty-one grandchildren, which is a rather small number for an OOM family.

Soon after the family's arrival in Columbiana, my mother began attending Germantown Road School (at the corner of Reckenberger Road). As mentioned earlier, this one-room schoolhouse served their Mennonite community until it closed in 1943, the year I would have attended first grade.

When in her teens, mother felt unsettled with the Old Order Mennonite religion. She began attending the less strict Midway Mennonite church. Midway had Sunday School—and other religious activities that engaged minds of thirsty young people who wanted to learn about the Bible and God. Midway also had a lenient dress code.

My maternal grandparents were not pleased with mother's "fancy" dresses. In fact, they forbade her to bring those "sinful things" into their home. My mother, in order to keep the peace with her parents, kept her dresses in the chicken hatchery, and changed there when attending Midway's functions.

When cars entered the world scene, members of the OOM "White" Church wanted to ditch their required horse-and-buggy means of transportation, and wanted to purchase cars. They petitioned their district bishop and asked him to make a change in church requirements. He approved cars on condition that the members paint the chrome bumpers black. This decision caused loud squawking by some church members, resulting in a schism within the White Church. My mother's parents joined the squawkers. They wanted nothing to do with cars, whether with black-bumpers or bumper-less, and returned to their home in Dayton, Virginia, where members still used the horse and buggy.

My mother stayed on in Columbiana, however, and worked in the home of my father's parents. Respect between my father and mother grew into infatuation, and they began to court. Mother, however, developed goiter, a condition caused by lack of iodine in one's system, which was common before iodized salt. Her goiter illness forced her return to Virginia, where she underwent surgery, and then was cared for by her parents. When at her frailest, her mother (my eventual grandmother) convinced her that she needed to rejoin the Old Order Mennonite religion.

My father loved my mother, and wrote frequent love letters, encouraging her to get well. In one of his letters he proposed, and my mother readily accepted. In the last few days of September, 1931, my father drove his 1926 Ford car to Virginia. They were soon married by a judge.

In attendance at my parents' marriage was my maternal grandfather, but not my maternal grandmother. Grandmother protested the marriage on the basis that an Old Order cannot marry a New Order, according to God's plan. "New" simply wasn't the true religion.

But *new* was all around, if grandmother had only opened her eyes. The *new*lyweds, my father and mother, returned to Columbiana and purchased a fairly *new* house on Germantown Road. Eight *new* children were conceived and born in that home. My father became ill with multiple sclerosis in that home, and was bedfast for seven years in the very bedroom where his children had been conceived.

My parents were happy together, except for *Old* and *New*. You'd think that since Mennonites are known as peaceful people, silly childish labels would have melted away in a marriage. Instead of melting, however, those labels became a stone weight that dragged upon their marriage.

You would also think that since my maternal grandmother lived in Virginia and my parents lived in Ohio, the distance in miles would have prevented grandmother from meddling into my parents' marriage. But such was not true.

Monitoring was accomplished through letters. The telephone, banned by the religion, was never missed by OOM women. They partook in letter-writing as frequently as one would make phone calls. Letters flew so quickly between their boxes that a mailman was alarmed if he had nothing to deliver.

My mother was the daughter living out-of-state. Grandma had sisters, another daughter, aunts and uncles, and friends galore living within the area that encircled the "White" Church. If mother dressed her girls in anything but black stockings, letters reporting such behavior were written that very night. They arrived in Grandma's mailbox in short order. She acted quickly, and wrote a particularly chastising letter, which reached my mother within the week.

Grandma Rhodes died in 1941, ten years after my parents had married. For remaining loyal, which meant continuing to dress her daughters the plain way, mother received a nice monetary inheritance. Can you imagine what this inheritance meant to a woman who had never been able to keep her own money? With her inheritance, mother purchased items that made her life easier. She purchased a motor that she attached to her Singer treadle sewing machine, easing her many stitching jobs. And she purchased a refrigerator so that we could get rid of our old ice box.

The above information is a rich documentation of change over time. These changes are:

Mother is born in Virginia and relocates to Ohio because of weather conditions. She is the fourth girl, and has two younger brothers, who never make it out of childhood, due to diseases caught en route to Ohio.

Her move to Ohio places my mother near my father's farm. The two fall in love, marry, and have eight children. I am the fifth child, and I have tried to document our story in my memoirs.

My mother loved documenting her days, as well. She called her documentary a diary. She was forty-nine when she changed Christian religions. Shortly after arriving in Akron in 1955 she began keeping a diary so that she could track her religious pilgrimage. She continued her diary until she died in 1989, at the age of eighty-three.

Pilgrims, being of Calvinistic persuasion, utilized the diary as a way of accounting for their days. As business owners track financial well-being by keeping daily notes of their revenues and expenses, the pilgrim tracks spiritual well-being and assesses moral progress by writing daily notes.

A pilgrim (and a Calvinist) believes that God put us upon this earth, and that we will rejoin God upon our death. "We are just passing through," mother often reminded her children. In the meantime, we were to live a fruitful and moral life, one that was pleasing to God.

As frequently mentioned in this book, mother's favorite writer of all times was John Bunyan. Bunyan, while imprisoned, wrote *The Pilgrim's Progress*, a diary of sorts, that documented the life of a man named Christian. Christian's perilous travels through earth's dangers were chronicled, chapter by chapter, as he journeyed to his heavenly home.

Considering that *Pilgrim's Progress* was mother's all-time favorite book, it does not surprise me that she chose the diary as her medium to account for her life. Daily notes chronicled activities, her personal conclusions of how she measured up thus far, and resolutions of what still needed to be accomplished. She also noted daily temperatures, weather conditions, and her personal weight.

Documenting the daily temperature and weather conditions serves as an accounting of one's environment. As such, diaries can be compared to tree rings. Trees track environmental conditions over time, and record such happenings in their wooden structures. The different colorations are like words on a page, and tell the tree's stories of how and when they experienced droughts, floods, optimal growing conditions, etc.

Documenting daily weight satisfied mother's quest for personal perfection, which she viewed as thin. Documenting her daily accomplishments met her guiding motto: *Life is short and one should not waste a single moment of a day in idleness.*

Unfortunately, mother's daily entries documented more failures than successes. An example is:

> *Maybe I should give God three hours of prayer each day for awhile, for my children are not as faithful as they should be. Some seem to have completely deserted the straight and narrow pathway. If God came today, they would not be ready.*

Her anguish led to action. She gave God even more hours of prayer each day. She called the church more frequently and requested prayer for her children. She paid extra tithes as suggested by her church.

The four revolutionary words, *Live and Let Live,* may have idealized mother's passion for religious independence, but did not free her from personal bondage.

Mother pitied people who were not saved and cried for them in her prayers. She could not bear to think of others burning in Hell. She wanted to help the poor and the down-and-out. She wanted to heal the sick. She wanted the disabled to throw away their crutches and ditch their wheelchairs. She wanted to see them walk again. She wanted to be the Evangelist who could do all these things, but the thought of speaking in front of groups filled her with fear.

Plaques with forget-me-knots saying "live and let live"—could not melt her childhood teachings. And mother never became the evangelist she felt called upon to be.

But mother was made powerful through pure determination, and set her feet upon a path whereby she could tell others about her love for God. If she couldn't be the evangelist who preached to the thousands, she could stand on street corners and minister to the few. She could pass out tracts and give personal testimony of what God had done for her. She could do that—and she would do that. The few that approached would not leave without a tract in hand. When she added up the numerous days that she stood at street corners passing out tracts, and the numerous tracts that had slipped from her hand into others, it added up to thousands, probably more. She accounted for all in her diary.

Also, documented in mother's diaries were her church habits. Her diaries described her quest for healings. Mother had never equated illness to being out of God's graces until she met Rev. Angley, the pastor of Grace Cathedral in Akron, Ohio. She had never known that to get back into God's good graces, one must fast.

Mother fasted to achieve her healing, but she'd get sicker and have to go to Rev. Angley for prayer. He'd pray, and she'd feel better—for a few days that is—then she felt a need to fast again.

Rev. Angley advocated fasting for other purposes as well. Fasting, which is the withholding of food, is a discipline practiced by many religions as a way of achieving a higher level of spiritual purity. Rev. Angley acknowledged that he had fasted forty days—as Jesus did.

Mother wanted to achieve a higher level of spiritual purity as well, so she tried fasting for days. But she would get ill and have to go to church for prayer. The cycle continued until she remembered a pilgrim-robot proverb that said: *The best way to tackle a big job is to do a little every day.* She fasted two days in one week, three days in another, noting all in her diary. Steadfastly, little by little, she stacked up the days until she reached forty. What a day of celebration that was! She had accomplished what Rev. Angley and Jesus had done. She circled her achievement with a red pen in her diary.

Mother bragged about her accomplishment to her children. What did it matter if she had adopted the walk of a turtle by fasting a few days a week—instead of the run of a rabbit by completing the entire forty days in one huge hop-swoop? She had reached the finish line, just the same. And her children didn't care one little bit, either. We just wanted a healthy and happy mother.

Unfortunately, mother's search for perfect health never ended in happy rabbit-turtle finishes. Her never-ending quest for spiritual perfection, her desire to be good, her need for the pat on the head, her need for more valium-hymns, soon appeared in another illness. She repeated her routine: Call Rev. Angley for prayer . . . need healing from illness . . . Rev. Angley names her illness . . . asks her to come to his service . . . asks her to testify about what God had done for her.

At times Rev. Angley names her illness nephritis. At other times he suggests congestive heart failure. At another time, he calls it pernicious anemia. It always has a name. "Just come to the service and be healed," Rev. Angley coaches. "Tell everyone what God has done for you."

My mother, elatedly, told her children about her healings. Down her fingers she'd go as she ticked off her illnesses, citing the day, month and year she had received each healing. When she finished her finger-tracking exercise, she shouted loudly: "Hallelujah!" and "Praise God!"

Sadly, mother's healings never lasted. Then, back to Rev. Angley she'd go and repeated the cycle. Her "need" made her totally dependent upon Rev. Angley. Ironically, passivity and total dependency were characteristics mother practiced daily when she was an Old Order Mennonite.

My mother may have needed healings, but being pointed out and made to feel special *were* **not** things mother received as an Old Order Mennonite. *Hmmm! Is that so?*

Quite the opposite occurred. *Hmmm!*

Pride was a thing of the devil! *Hmmm!*

Never mind believing that our religion was unique and that God favored us above all others. *Hmmm!*

Never mind believing that we were the only people who were good enough to go to heaven when we died. *Hmmm!*

Never mind that all we needed do was stay on the straight and narrow pathway, isolated, never looking left or right! *Hmmm!*

Never mind that we were the "pointed-out" pilgrims in our different dress and with our strange behaviors. *Hmmm! Hmmm! Hmmm!*

Never mind that we grew up on valium hymns. *Hmmm! Hmmm! Hmmm! Hmmm!!*

Elitism, the belief that God loved us best, certainly made us feel good and made us feel valued—and yes, even superior. Most importantly, it gave us the resolve to plant our feet upon that straight and narrow pathway that led to our heavenly home.

My mother's diaries documented a story of change over time. She frequently described her difficulty with hairdressers. My sisters and I empathized with her perplexing situations, for we experienced much distress, as well. According to the Scriptures, OOM women were taught that their hair was never to be cut. And we were taught to be meek and humble, and to serve others rather than be served. Therefore, to visit a beauty parlor and to be served by others was a disconcerting experience. Yet, when in Rome, you do what the Romans do, or . . . perish.

We frequented beauty parlors, having our hair cut, colored, and curled, soon after our arrival in the big City. Beauty establishments were strange places for us. How did we know what to ask for? With low self esteem, we couldn't ask for advice, fearing we'd appear dumb. Therefore, we settled for unsettledness, and allowed the hairdresser to do her/his thing.

An hour later, when presented with the results, we gasped inwardly, an action most of the world cannot do, but stoic people can do splendidly well. We never complained, thereby maintaining our pilgrim upbringing without actually walking the path. We even managed a generous tip when we paid the bill, and agreed to a second appointment in a month.

In mother's diaries, she eloquently described her beauty-shop distress. Displeased with the cut, the color, and hairstyle, she was unable to voice her displeasure. Indeed, upon departure, she complimented the hairdresser, and even left a generous tip. *Yeah! We know all about this, my sisters and I could say.*

She even made a new appointment before leaving the shop. *Yeah!—yeah! We know about this, too.*

For the next few days, she wrestled with her displeasure. She would have called and canceled the scheduled appointment, if she could have offered an appropriate excuse? *La-de-da! La-de-da! Creativity rather than passivity required here.*

Telling the truth would surely have offended the hairdresser. *Poor hairdresser! She'd just die from the stress!*

This would be a confrontation. *Oh dear!*

Telling an untruth, such as finding a hairdresser closer by, would be a lie. *Mother, take it from me: Better to confess than to stress!*

Her only alternative was to return for her scheduled appointment and hope for the best. *Okay! Not the best way! But it buys you another day. Sometimes it's the only thing you can do.*

Reasons mother and her daughters could not honestly speak to their hairdresser about their displeasure are:

(1) We can't confront or speak up for ourselves, not even to express displeasure with our hair-do.

(2) Our behavior is representational of children groomed to be pleasers.

(3) Our behavior shows our low self-esteem: we don't want our hairdresser to think we're dumb.

(4) Our behavior shows our extreme fragility: We can't handle denouncements or angry responses; and, therefore, patronize behaviors that harm us.

All four statements describe the reasons for our behavior. But these are childish behaviors! When I became an adult, I put away my childish things, did I not?

Some of mother's diary entries revealed her obsessive-compulsive qualities, as in the following examples:

(1) Mom believed cleanliness was next to godliness. She frequently mopped her apartment, diligently cleaning every corner. She was not content until each and every speck of dirt floated or settled in her wash bucket.

Her zest for cleanliness was not limited to her apartment floors, however. She had a lovely balcony, which needed frequent scrubbings. She lived on the tenth floor of her seniors' apartment building, which meant nine balconies were located below.

She had her special way of cleaning her balcony. First, she filled her bucket with warm water and poured it, all at once, onto her balcony floor. Then she scrubbed and scrubbed her wet balcony floor. Apparently, she didn't think about the people living below, or that the excess water slouching off her balcony would drip onto their balconies. Residents of these apartments complained loudly. "This gush of water suddenly flowed onto my balcony!" they angrily complained to the apartment manager. "Tell her to quit!" The office told mother to stop.

But mother, behaving like the obsessive-compulsive robot she had been trained to be, devised a clever solution. She set her alarm clock for two A.M. In this early morning hour, when normal people slept, she arose and poured warm water onto her balcony. Only the moon and stars were awake to view her activity. Astonished, they assigned her activities to "None of our business!"—continuing their heavenly chores. Meanwhile, mother happily scrubbed and scrubbed her balcony floor.

Rainy days made her even happier, for the outpouring of rain meant she could now fool her neighbors in apartments below. She filled her bucket with warm water, and then poured it onto her balcony floor. She scrubbed and scrubbed to her heart's delight, secure in her belief that neighbors below would simply think the sudden gush of water was an outburst of rain.

(2) My mother's most horrifying obsession was with cockroaches. She never had roaches before moving into the senior's apartment building, and blamed them on her "dirty neighbors"—her words. Seeing her first roach sent her on a search-and-destroy mission. She searched every corner, nook and cranny with her flashlight. "The only good roach is a dead roach," she told her children. We knew this to be true, for we saw her eyes glass over when a roach darted across her floor. In murderous rage, she'd grab a fly swatter, roll up a newspaper, take off her shoe—anything that she could use that was quick, convenient, and cut easily through air. One fast, deadly whack was all she intended to deliver. Her proof was in the pudding, for there on the floor would lie the roach, feet in the air, hardly visible with a body now flatter than a crepe.

Roach frustration led mother to an intelligent conclusion, one that greatest biologists have yet to learn. "Both male and female roaches can have babies," she would say to her children with straightest of face. "Did you know that?" She'd wait for a moment, and when unable to hold frivolity any longer, she'd erupt into raucous laughter. This was our clue that stuff was not up to snuff, and we eyed our mother, suspiciously. Our mother, however, was pleased that she had fooled her children. I think you'll agree it's a pretty funny joke. Remarkably, mother had created this levity out of extreme frustration.

(3) Another obsession of mother's was shopping. When I first began reading her diary, I was amazed at the numerous trips she made downtown to buy a new dress, shoes, purses, finest face creams, a fur hat, etc.

How could you, Mom? I quietly questioned. Do you not remember that you allowed your daughters only two dresses a school year, and your sons were allowed only two shirts and two pants? It seemed mother, freely and flippantly, now purchased dresses on the slightest whim. However, I knew if I questioned her strange behavior, she would have replied most innocently, "Why, Esther May, I need these dresses for church. God wants His children to look nice when they sit in His pews. Rev. Angley says God's children deserve the finest."

(4) Frequently, mother's diaries detailed frustrating gossip situations with neighbors in her senior's apartment building. Rev. Angley warned his

members about the dangers of mingling, and especially about the dangers of gossip. "It uses up valuable time that could better be used in reading God's word and in prayer," he told his followers.

When the first knocks arrived on mother's door, she welcomed the visitor. The visitor delivered juicy gossip, as fresh as hand-picked flowers, and mother was as giddy as a child. This attention made her feel special, valued, as if she had finally arrived—and could now be the girl in the loop instead of the pilgrim who walked alone.

The knocks occurred more frequently. Her neighbor would rush in telling stories that smashed other tenants, smashed them as mother did her roaches. "You know, Jane, the bleached blond who lives upstairs? Imagine bleaching your hair when you're gray! Jane entertained a new suitor last evening. If you ask me, Jane's not that cute, if you get my drift, so she must be putting out, or putting in, ha! ha! ha!—if you get my drift, ha! ha! ha!" Such gossip wore on my mother, upsetting her for days. Yet she couldn't confront the gossiper and tell her to stop coming around. She couldn't do that.

Because she couldn't ask her neighbor to stop coming to her door, mother resorted to secretive behavior. She hid in her apartment. When the neighbor knocked, pretending she wasn't home, she didn't answer the door. At times her television played when the knocks arrived, requiring that she tippy-toe across her room to shut it off. Then, afraid that her friend might have heard her footsteps, or the television noise, she fretted, the distress filling her stomach with acid.

She hated her sneaky behavior, but didn't have enough self-esteem to tell her neighbor to stop. Finally, unable to handle unsettledness, which bred like bacteria within her, she visited her neighbor. "Did you knock? she asked most innocently. "Did you come by for a visit?" Naturally, this restarted the visitations and knocks upon her door.

Overwhelmed once more, mother resorted to slipping notes under her offending neighbor's door. *Please, don't come visit me anymore. I am to give Rev. Angley even more time in prayer, which is not to be interrupted. And I have to copy sermon notes for an ill person now, someone who can't go to church anymore. With my own notes, and now notes for this sick lady, I have more than I can handle. So please, don't knock on my door anymore. I'll be sure to say hello if by chance we meet in the hall or laundry room.*

(5) My mother, because she couldn't confront, put notes under doors for other reasons as well. For instance, noticing she had an excess of bird dirt

on her balcony floor, accused the lady living in the apartment above of feeding the birds. Without identifying herself, she wrote a note, asking the lady to not do this anymore. It did nothing to solve the problem, as you might imagine.

(6) Another problem that bugged mother was her hard-of-hearing neighbor, Sunny. Because of Sunny's hearing condition, Sunny set her television volume too loudly. My mother diligently recorded the television irritations and noted the times in her diary. *It's 8:45 AM, television too loud. 9: 31 AM now, television still too loud. Put note under Sunny's door about it. 10:20 AM now. Television is still too loud.*

For days and weeks the monitoring continued, with complaints and times recorded in her diary. Intermittent notes were slid under Sunny's door, my mother recording these times as well.

Perhaps you can understand at this point why a pilgrim must walk alone all the days of his/her life.

(7) Pilgrims self-sacrifice to the point that it hurts, and many hurting people belong to cults. In order to get a valium lift, hurting people will give freely of their money in offerings. Cult leaders seem to have a special knack for identifying self-sacrificing people.

When mother moved to Akron in 1955, she purchased a large home on the North Side of Akron. She certainly had to watch her pennies, but gave freely to Rev. Rex Humbard. Once, when he cried the blues about going broke, she gave him two-thousand dollars. To his credit, he knew she couldn't afford that much money, and tried to give it back. But Mother would have none of this. She told Reverend Rex that God had told her to give him that money, and emphatically stated, "Whatever God tells someone to do, they had better do it!"

Years later, after selling her North Hill home and living off Social Security Income, she listened to Rev. Angley's tales of woe. She gave too much money again. At that time, Rev. Angley had traveled to Europe, and had gotten into trouble with political leaders in Germany. Fearing jail, he made tear-drenching pleas to church members. "Give 'til you hurt," he said, "and God will be pleased and reward you greatly." Mother was moved by his plea, and sent Angley a check for three-hundred dollars. The trouble was she had no more than thirty dollars in her checking account.

"Give us all of your money. Give 'til it hurts." I wonder how many cult members have answered such pleas, simply because of their need to medicate unworthy feelings. And I wonder how many of them become wards of the government?

Daily, our lives are affected by changes. The automobile is a great example of change. Before the 1900s, country-sides and cities were vastly different from what they are today.

When the automobile first appeared on streets and in garages, people viewed this strange metal-on-wheels with awe. Supper conversations circled around the car. Uncle Joe told the story about his Ford leaving him stranded, and that he had to walk into his pasture and ride one of his cows home. Cousin Samuel said his car broke down while traveling along some country road. Fortunately, another car came along, and that driver helped him out. And, even more fortunately, the driver had a beautiful daughter with him, whom he eventually married.

Most car conversations broke into happy laughter as teenage boys told of the pleasure of driving for the first time, alone, without Papa knowing, and of grandma telling how the wind blew off her hat and she hasn't seen it since.

Through our senses of seeing, hearing, touching, and smelling, we adapted to the changes that automobiles brought into our lives. Now, they are commonplace.

As we have progressed through time—into the twentieth century—and into the twenty-first—cell phones and computers, with their ever-changing complexities, have replaced the automobile in supper conversations. Indeed, cell phones have changed the very way supper-table conversations are handled. One diner might chat happily with a nearby chair companion, while another diner communicates with a friend thousands of miles away. Silent text messages have replaced vocal conversations.

It's hard to fathom where all of this will go; it's hard to predict what changes will dominate future supper-table conversations. Perhaps a bright son or daughter might finally explain near-death experiences, where one's own body floats above one's other body. Perhaps another bright son or daughter will connect dreams to our photographic childhood memories.

Whatever our bright children come up with, it will be different from what we are experiencing today. And supper-table conversations will reflect these changes.

We may lament and wish we were trees, for then the environmental changes that automobiles brought onto our landscape could have been recorded in "our" rings. Alas, we're not trees, and, we have no rings. Sadly, all that information is gone. Not so! Not so by a long shot! All environmental changes are written somewhere.

Most phenomenal are the environmental changes that take a seat at our supper table. What one eats today reflects the changes of yesterdays. You did not have to kill the chicken for today's supper, but simply purchased it already processed for you at your nearby grocery store.

You did not pick the fresh beans from your garden, but simply purchased them at the grocery, and had a choice of frozen or fresh. The butter you spread on your bread did not come from the cow grazing in your nearby meadow. In fact, if you looked out your kitchen window, you'd not see a garden, or a chicken coop, or a pig pen, or a meadow, or a barn filled with cows. You'd not even see a meadow with peach and apple trees.

It's most likely that your children don't even know where the food they consume originates, other than at the local grocery or fast-food eatery. We may not have tree rings that document such changes, but, if you look around, the changes that have taken place over time are written everywhere.

Changes show up in our diaries, are snapped in photographs, are recorded in historical documentaries, appear in educational media, are printed in literature, painted in art, and consumed in the multitude of media available to us. Ongoing technology will make the gathering of changes through time even more easily captured, stored, and retrieved. For that's what we seek, isn't it? We need to know where we've been so that we can see where we're going. What a wonderful way for intelligent beings to evolve!

Religious cultures, such as the OOM and their sister religions, who demand that their members live in the past, try their best to stop evolution. They refuse to use the automobile, but continue with the horse-and-buggy for transportation. How do these people manage to isolate themselves from evolutionary factors? Can they escape the big ball of evolution that has rolled over cultures for countless centuries?

The religious cultures of my childhood have always been in step with evolutionary time. Because of their limited education, they are unaware that they're in step, and might even view evolution negatively. But they're in step with evolution, all the same.

Amish and OOM's do not live in a vacuum. In order to make a living in our wonderful country, they have altered their milking barns to meet local, state and federal regulations. They are planting seeds genetically engineered. They use fertilizers and insecticides specifically manufactured to match the needs of the genetically-altered seeds. These adaptations to environmental changes are in present time, which is evolutionary time.

OOM and sister religions have always practiced genetic selection when it comes to their livestock. In their desire to have the finest and best animals for breeding, they have brought in superior horses, cows, sheep and chickens from near and far to mate with their stock. Since artificial insemination is now available and cheaper, they have readily changed over to this modern convenience. They have been rewarded with supreme animals that handsomely compete in the world's economic marketplace. All this activity is in evolutionary time, without doubt.

But when it comes to protecting their fair females' eggs, present time stops. Only proper DNA will be used now, and that proper DNA comes from their fathers, their forefathers, and from generations they trace back through generation and generation, farther than one can properly document without a DNA analysis. In their effort to keep their gene-line pure, their membership is required to step out of present time.

Isolation limits breeding possibilities, in the same way that Holstein cows and bulls that are penned together will have only Holstein calves. As a consequence, Amish children look like their parents. Through conditioning, Amish children act like their parents, believe like their parents, and perpetuate the same beliefs and lifestyle as did their past generations.

As far as evolution is concerned, one never knows who will write the next word. Will it be those who are computer savvy? Or will it be someone who knows how to farm? Will it be someone who genetically alters the seeds, or will it be someone who harvests seeds that have not been altered, those still using wild seeds, as they're called? Will it be someone who knows how to survive without the need of electricity or automobiles, and relies on the winds and the rains to make a living? Evolution will write our future as surely as it has written our past. Evolution always writes our last word.

Throughout my childhood years, my mother sang beautiful love songs to Jesus. They're called hymns, but some are love songs just the same. *Oh, How Sweet the Name of Jesus* is one such song. As mother began singing this song to her children, we joined in her trance. Her trembling voice hit each note perfectly, sending an emotional sweetness that shivered across our room.

Other frequently sung hymns were *Nearer My God to Thee*—and *The Lord my Shepherd is; I shall be well supplied; since he is mine and I am his, what can I want beside?* Within my family, hymns served as our communicator, and served as the communicator within our community and church. Hymns knit us together, socially and emotionally.

Some say music is the great communicator between members of a particular species. The songs of whales, the tweeting of birds, the sawing of grasshopper feet and the buzzing of the bees are examples of species' communication. Each species has its unique voice, and each seems to have the power to unite, delight, and comfort.

The voice that directed and delighted my childhood days was the valium hymns that mother sang around our house. Sometimes she communicated through warning hymns, such as: *Stop, poor sinner, stop and think, before you farther go. Will you sport upon the brink of everlasting woe?* Another warning song said: *Sinners, turn, why will ye die? God, your Maker, asks you why.*

Love songs to God were my favorites, which she belted out with such gusto that the framing of our house begged for mercy. *The Love of God, is greater far, than tongue of man, can ever tell.*

Frequently mother sang transporting hymns, words so beautiful they had the capacity to transport you to another place. An example of such a hymn is the well-loved song: *I come to the Garden alone, while the dew is still on the roses, and the joy we share as we tarry there, is like none other has ever known.*

When I entered my teenage years, mother taught me a song specifically meant to frighten me. The song went as follows: *Young people who, delight in sin, I'll tell you what, has lately been. A woman who was young and fair, she died in sin, and sad despair. She'd go to frolics, dance and plays, in spite of all, to friends, she'd say, I'll turn to God, when I get old. And he will then receive my soul.* There are thirteen verses to this song. The girl, naturally, gets sick and dies and her soul forever burns in hell.

I learned about God, Jesus and Heaven through the hymns mother sang in our home throughout the day. God was love; God was all-powerful; God saw everything; God punished you if you even thought about bad things; God controlled your life.

When I sang hymns with mother, we transcended the physical barriers that kept us rooted upon earth. Many churches conduct services intended to transcend their worshippers from their physical barriers, as well. The use of songs in altar calls, where one is "born again", is particularly well-known.

I have found nothing that equals the uplifting power of a good songfest, where one smiles to the one on the left and the one on the right, and the ones in the rows in front of you when they turn around and smile, and the ones in the rows behind you, when you pass the smile along.

The rave dances that I've seen on television seem to capture this sort of trance, as do the wave movements that engulf crowds at sport events. Political events have chants that seem to give valium highs, as do musical concerts of all sorts.

"Live and Let Live" is a plaque of peacefulness. In today's world pronouncements as to whether one is good or bad pour forth as freely as water pours over a dam. Good or bad pronouncements are words of discernment—words attributed to God—words appearing in the first book of the Bible. God saw everything He had made and pronounced it good. Genesis 1:31.

Words of discernment were used by Adam and Eve when they ate the fruit from the tree of knowledge. Eating this fruit allowed Adam and Eve to discern good from evil, or to know they were naked. Being naked was bad and they desired to be good, so clothed themselves through sewing fig leaves together, thereby making the first apron. From then on, human beings have been able to discern (or think for themselves). All this ability came to Adam and Eve, our first parents, and then into us, so we have been told.

Most of us are emotionally affected when a good or bad label is placed upon us. Such labels, seemingly, describe our very core. It's no wonder we need valium hymns to communicate.

"Live and Let Live" is a plaque of independence. Oddly, mother purchased this plaque when she felt the first breezes of freedom. Widowed for a short time, the breeze of independence, enticing as it was, convinced her that she needed a change in religion. Unfortunately, mother could not have known that the religion that encased her would not erase her need for valium. She moved from one supplier to another.

Throughout this book I have tried not to preach to you, for I know how unbecoming it is for pilgrims to do so. And I know cult members do nothing, but preach and discern. And I know martyrs are as inflexible as a stick. And I know that most religions preach that black is always black—and white is always white—and that truth is always truth—no matter what.

"I've found the true religion!" proclaimed mother when we made the big move to Akron, Ohio.

Each religion claims it alone owns the **truth.** Can absolute truth exist? It's more likely that truth evolves, that it changes over time to meet the social needs of the people.

People tend to stumble when walking on shifting sand. They need the permanence of rock. The Bible tells us about rock-solid truth, the truth God represents. Religions preach: *He is the same yesterday, today and tomorrow.* Religions are rarely the same yesterday, today, and tomorrow—because people are not the same. Truth mirrors society's needs of the time. And, the plain truth is that society walks on shifting sand because of changing environments.

Social needs change because environmental conditions change. Sicknesses, wars, political and religious powers, increases in populations, inventions allowing free time, more hours of play, are factors that comprise the shifting sands of social needs. As Peter, Paul and Mary sang in the sixties: *The times, they are a changing.*

Religious groups that buck the winds of change by making their people live in the past, by having as many children as they please, will affect evolution—but will not halt evolution. Evolution is greater than human beings. Evolution is about the plant and animal species that inhabit our earth. As one species is harmed, another flourishes.

Evolution's whirling winds encompass changes in space, changes in weather, and changes in how much rock and how much sand we have upon earth. Some things are impossible to buck.

A tree writes all environmental changes that take place in its rings. A tree **can't** look at its rings and say, "I need to spend more hours a day facing southward so that my seeds will be more robust and more will survive."

But human beings can reflect upon what has happened in the past. They do so in cultures, and they do so in cults. They do so in religions, in nationalities, and in countless other social groups. They do so because they want more of their seeds to face southward, and they do so because they need to harness the harsh winds from the north. They do so because if their progeny doesn't survive, nothing else in life is worth pursuing.

I think my father had it right: *God moves in mysterious ways, His wonders to perform.*

The End

EPILOGUE

As a young girl, when I complained about having to live such a harsh way of life because of my religion, mother answered my complaints by saying, "Esther May, we're just pilgrims passing through this world on our way to our heavenly home. If you think of it in this way, it'll be much easier for you to accept."

As a child I accepted her explanations. And, if I had stayed within the Old Order Mennonite religion, I would have continued to accept her explanations, for I had no other course but to walk my pilgrim pathway. I knew nothing else, and would learn nothing else, because my religion limited my education and exposure to the outside world.

As a result, I grew up in pilgrim-past—with all the other people who grew up in pilgrim-past. We comprised a pocket of people who were required to live out-of-time in a controlled, static environment. We worked hard and mingled little with the outside world, whom we had been taught to fear. As such, our religion can be defined as a cult.

Throughout the centuries, cults have come dressed as religions, as cultures, as nationalities, and as societies. Members of cults are taught through words, songs and rituals in messages that say: "We are the true people; we are the true way. Follow us upon earth and you'll live forever in heaven."

Today, if my mother said to me, "We are just Pilgrims passing through this world, on our way to our heavenly home," I would say to her, "Yes, we are mother. Yes we are.

"I wanted to learn in my life, and you made learning possible when you moved us out of the Old Order Mennonite religion. I wanted to learn who we were.

"I learned that, indeed, we were born lonely pilgrims; and that we grew up as lonely pilgrims. As children, early on, we got stuck in Dr. Erikson's "stages"—which left us as children for the rest of our lives. We became the child-adult who said, 'I like my hairdo. Thank you very much. And, here's an extra tip.' We just never could get beyond that stage.

"We had many harsh rules and regulations, but the one that harmed us most was the OOM's stringent non-confrontation policy. When others tease you or hurt you, you have to just stand there and take it. Don't speak up for yourself, and don't fight back."

As Dr. Eric Erikson postulated in his "Eight Stages in Life", you can grow up in body, but still remain a child.

Until they awaken
they will never know who they are.
And until they know who they are,
They can never awaken.

ACKNOWLEDGMENTS

I am most grateful to my third cousin, Fred Gerlach, for early editing and advice on *Girls in the Cult.* I thank my husband, Jim Ayers, and my author-friend Dick Kelly, for wise advice as I prepared my book for publishing. I thank Alexis Powers and the Oro Valley Workshop for Writers' attendees for listening to me read parts of this book, for offering suggestions, and for keeping me strong.

I am most grateful to all who have read my sister book—*Rolling Down Black Stockings*—and offered great comments that spurred me think deeper. You were right: I had another book within me.

And, as always, I am most grateful to my sons, their wives, and my grandsons for being my biggest cheerleaders in life. Thanks for your enduring confidence and love.

BOOKS BY THE AUTHOR

Ayers, Esther Royer. *Rolling Down Black Stockings.* Kent and London: Kent State University Press, 2005. Non-fiction Memoir

Oberlin, Sarah Blosser, with Esther Royer Ayers. *A Heritage That Money Can't Buy: My Growing Up Years as an Old Order Mennonite.* Florida: CasAnanda Publishing, 1997. Non-fiction Memoir

Ayers, Esther Royer. *Flights of the Herons.* Xlibris Corporation (www.Xlibris.com), 2001. Fiction—with actual Reyher genealogy information.

Books recommended by author for additional information:

Estep, William R. *The Anabaptist Story: An Introduction to Sixteenth-Century Anabaptism,* 3rd Edition, Revised & Enlarged. Wm. B. Eerdman's Publishing Co. Grand Rapids/Cambridge, 1996.

Kraybill, Donald B. and C. Nelson Hostetter. *Anabaptist World USA.* Herald Press. Pennsylvania, 2001.

Kraybill, Donald B. (Text) and Niemeyer, Lucian (Photographs) *Old Order Amish: Their Enduring Way of Life.* The Johns Hopkins University Press, Baltimore and London, 1993. [This book's colorful cover mentioned in Chapter 2]

Brunk, Harry Anthony. *History of Mennonites in Virginia 1727-1900.* Virginia Book Company, 1959. [Book mentioned in Chapter 1—for it describes how the Old Order Mennonite name came about]

http://www.gameo.org/encyclopedia/contents/O544.html will give you information about Old Order Mennonites in Virginia during the time of the Jacob Wisler schism.

Armstrong, Karen. *The Spiral Staircase: My Climb Out of Darkness.* New York—Toronto: Alfred A. Knopf, 2004.

Tobias, Madeleine Landau and Janja Lalich. *Captive Hearts Captive Minds: Freedom and Recovery from Cults and Abusive Relationships.* Almeda, California: Hunter House Inc. Publishers, 1994.

Hymnals—Song Books:

Mennonite Hymns. A collection of Psalms and Hymns, suited to the various occasions of public worship. Compiled by a number of Old Order Mennonite Brethren. 1928. The Ruebush-Kieffer Co., Dayton, VA.

Church Hymnal—Mennonite. Acquired by our family in 1951, when I was thirteen.

Eric H. Erickson's *Eight Stages of Life*—Used as a guide in this book.

1. Trust or Mistrust—Birth to 18 Months
2. Confidence or Doubt—18 Months to 4 Years
3. Initiative or Guilt—Years 4 to 6
4. Industry or Inferiority—Years 6 to 12
5. Identity or Confusion—Years 12 to 18
6. Intimacy or Isolation—Years 18 to 25
7. Growth or Stagnation—Years 25 to 40
8. Integrity or Despair—Years 40 and Beyond

BIBLIOGRAPHY

1   Bunyan, John.   *The Pilgrim's Progress.*   (See numerous Internet sources regarding this book.

2   Singer, Margaret Thaler.   *Cults in Our Midst.*   San Francisco: Jossey-Bass Publishers, 1995.

3   van Braght, Thieleman J. (with illustrations by Jan Luyken). *Martyr's Mirror: The Story of Seventeen Centuries of Christian Martyrdom, From the Time of Christ to A.D.* Scottsdale, PA. & Waterloo, Ontario: Herald Press, 1660.

4   Erikson, Erik H.   *Childhood and Society: 35th Anniversary Edition. New York—London:* W. W. Norton & Company, 1985.

5   Armstrong, Karen. *Through the Narrow Gate: A Memoir of Spiritual Discovery.* New York: St. Martin's Press, 1981.

6   *Amish in the City.* A television reality show produced by UPN, 2004. (Google or Yahoo, or use another Search Engine for additional information.)

7   Friedan, Betty. *The Feminine Mystique.*   New York: *W.W.Norton andCo., 1963.*

8   Athens, Lonnie. *Violent Criminal Acts and Actors Revisted.*   Urbana and Chicago: University of Illinois Press, 1997.

9   Rhodes, Richard. *Why They Kill: The Discoveries of a Maverick Criminologist.* New York: Vintage Books, A Division of Random House, Inc., 1999.

Made in the USA
Lexington, KY
08 December 2014